PAINLESS
Spelling

Mary Elizabeth Podhaizer, M.Ed.

illustrated by Hank Morehouse

BARRON'S

All inquiries should be addressed to:
Barron's Educational Series, Inc.
250 Wireless Boulevard
Hauppauge, New York 11788
http://www.barronseduc.com

Library of Congress Catalog Card No.: 98-18313

International Standard Book No. 0-7641-0567-1

Library of Congress Cataloging-in-Publication Data

Podhaizer, Mary Elizabeth.
    Painless spelling / Mary Elizabeth Podhaizer ; illustrated by
Hank Morehouse.
        p.   cm.
    Includes index.
    Summary: Provides guidelines for spelling American English words;
explains visual and sound patterns, letter combinations, syllables,
compound words, and hyphenation; and includes practical exercises.
    ISBN 0-7641-0567-1
    1. English language—Orthography and spelling—Study and
teaching (Elementary)—Juvenile literature.   2. English language—
Orthography and spelling—Study and teaching (Middle school)—
Juvenile literature.   [1. English language—Spelling.
2. Vocabulary.]   I. Morehouse, Hank, ill.   II. Title.
LB1574.P63   1998
372.63´2—dc21   98-18313
                                                                          CIP
                                                                          AC

PRINTED IN THE UNITED STATES OF AMERICA
9 8 7 6 5 4 3 2

This book is for Fr. Paa Kwesi Maison
and everyone—
born in America or elsewhere—
who tries to make sense of
English spelling.

Acknowledgments

Thank you to the authors of *Words Their Way: Word Study for Phonics, Vocabulary, and Spelling Instruction*, whose intelligent and insightful developmental approach to spelling provided the categories around which I organized this book.

CONTENTS

INTRODUCTION

Which is correct: *cosily* or *cozily*? *theater* or *theatre*? *traveler* or *traveller*? The answer may surprise you: they are ALL correct. And that's the first problem with spelling in English— sometimes there's more than one correct way to write a word. But that's only the beginning. Teeming with words from other languages, English can seem like an impossible language to spell correctly. Not to worry. This book will take you on a tour of American English and help you nail down the basics that will make spelling most English words less of a challenge.

Sure, you'll still run across words that are exceptions to the rules you learn. And one of the main reasons for this is that, for practical purposes, any word in an American English dictionary, no matter what its origin, is considered English, and as a result, we have to work with spelling rules from many different languages of origin. For example, if you want to spell *qiviut*, the Inuit word for the undercoat of the musk ox, you have to ignore the rule that *q* is always followed by *u*. But for the most part, the

Qiviut!

guidelines in this book will help you steer cleanly through the inconsistencies of the strange and wonderful language we call English. (The dictionary we'll be using as our point of reference, unless otherwise noted, is *The American Heritage Dictionary of the English Language*.)

These days, some folks are saying that spelling is not very important. They argue that since most people do most of their writing on a computer, and using the spell checker is a cinch, we don't need to focus on spelling. Don't get taken in by this reasoning! If you type *through* instead of *threw,* or *their* instead of *there,* or *even* instead of *event,* your spell checker can't tell that you made a mistake—all six are perfectly good and correctly spelled English words. One study found that as many as 40 percent of spelling errors are real-word errors in which one word is mistakenly typed for another. In addition, if you type *eggzasparated* instead of *exasperated,* your spell checker may not have a clue about what word you MEANT to type (mine didn't!). And if you're walking by the sporting goods store and see that they're holding interviews today, and you have to fill out a job application for them, you won't get a chance to spell-check your writing. The people who are doing the hiring will judge you on your spelling, among other things. You'll want to be prepared with a good, broad knowledge of how to spell English words.

The fact is, no matter how many gadgets and gizmos you have to help you, you still need to know fundamental spelling rules in order to communicate with people. And that's the whole point! We don't learn spelling rules for the sake of learning the rules. The goal is to express ourselves in a way that others can understand. THAT'S the reason to learn to spell.

We begin with talking about visual and sound patterns in English. Then we go on a tour of the patterns to help you learn or review the combinations you see and hear every day. The exercises will help you see the relationships between spoken and written language and become more aware of the structure of written words and the relationships between and among words. They will also help you become more familiar with the characteristic patterns of English spelling. You can jot down your answers to the exercises on loose-leaf paper or in a notebook. By the time we're finished, you'll be able to spend more time thinking about what you're communicating instead of how to spell it correctly. And that's where it's at!

THE HISTORY OF ENGLISH

Do you know what a mongrel is? Sometimes we use the word *mongrel* to refer to a dog with a mixed background. So you can think of it as meaning "a mixture." The English language is a mixture in this sense.

The English language came into being around 450 A.D. Three tribes from Northern Europe—the Angles, the Saxons, and the Jutes—invaded the British Isles. The main island came to be known as jolly old "Angle"land (England), and the language that came into being became known as Anglo-Saxon or **Old English**. Every one of the top 100 most frequently used words in English today comes from Old English.

BRAIN TICKLERS
Set # 1

Hey, that was some generalization about the top 100 words in English! What are the most frequently used words in English, anyway? And do they really come from Old English? To check it out yourself, follow these directions.

1. Choose one page of text in a book (any book you like—as long as it's written in English, that is).

2. Count how many times each word appears and keep tabs. You might want to use tally marks. This won't exactly give you the top 100 most frequently used words in English, but it will give you an idea of some words that are used pretty often.

3. Look up the most frequently used words in a dictionary. Check out the etymological information in the entry (the part that tells what language the word comes from).

4. Compare your findings with those of your classmates, if possible.

(Answers are on page xv.)

Getting back to the history of English . . . In about 600 A.D., the language began to change because St. Augustine came to Britain, bringing Christianity and a lot of Latin words. People started learning to write English, and so English spelling was invented.

But then more invasions brought more new words into English. The Vikings arrived in the late 700s bringing Danish words. And then in 1066 came William the Conqueror, bringing French words. After a couple of hundred years, the differences that resulted from the addition of French were so great that the change in the language has a name. We call the mixture of Old English with French that was spoken starting in the early 1200s **Middle English**. Just to let you know how that influence has lasted, about 40 percent of all English words used today have French origins.

The rediscovery of Greek and Latin classics in the period of the Renaissance (1300s–1600s) and the introduction of the printing press in the 1400s brought many new words to England. All these new additions to the language kept things very unsettled until the mid-1700s, when English spelling became standardized as the result of the publication of a definitive dictionary by Samuel Johnson—and this is when **Modern English** began.

But those aren't all the sources for English!! Not by a long shot. Here's a sampling of fairly common English words and their sources:

Word	Language of Origin	Word	Language of Origin
ketchup	Malay	tepee	Dakota
canyon	Spanish	wok	Chinese
skunk	Algonquian	futon	Japanese
matzo	Yiddish	chipmunk	Ojibwa
algebra	Arabic	boomerang	Dhaurk (Australian aborigine language)
yak	Tibetan	pizza	Italian

BRAIN TICKLERS
Set # 2

1. Look at this list of nine common English words that have come into English from another language. Use a dictionary to look up each word's etymology. The dictionary will begin with the language from which the word came most recently and work back to the language of ultimate origin. Briefly tell in what language the word began and how it traveled into English.

artichoke	boss	cooky or cookie	jungle	oboe
raccoon	robot	tea	teak	

2. Think of one word that you think came into English from another language. Check in a dictionary to see if you are right. Write down the language of ultimate origin.

(Answers are on page xv.)

Understanding a little about the sources of English will help you understand why there are different patterns of spelling in English. Each language of origin has its own rules for representing sounds with letters. In addition, the pronunciation of English has changed over time. So sounds are not represented by letters in English in a one-to-one correspondence. We'll talk more about this beginning in Chapter 2. This book will help you spell English words by calling your attention to the patterns of spelling and helping you understand what you can expect from English words.

BRAIN TICKLERS— THE ANSWERS

Set # 1, page xi

Answers will vary depending on the material you have chosen. The most frequently used word in this entire introduction (pages vii–xiv; 1,385 words) is (can you guess?) *the*. It appears 86 times. And guess what! It's from Old English. Here are some other frequently used words in this chapter—all from Old English.

of 50 times	**you** 34 times	**a** 30 times
English 44 times	**in** 33 times	**word** 23 times
to 40 times	**and** 31 times	**that** 21 times

Set # 2, page xiv

Answers may vary depending on the dictionary used.

1. **artichoke**   Arabic to Old Spanish to Italian to English
   boss   Germanic to Middle Dutch to Dutch to English
   cooky or cookie   Middle Dutch to Dutch to English
   jungle   Sanskrit to Hindi and Marathi to English
   oboe   French to Italian to English
   raccoon   Algonquian to English
   robot   Czech to English
   tea   Ancient Chinese to Amoy to Malay to Dutch to English
   teak   Malayalam to Portuguese to English

2. Answers will vary. Possible responses:

café Turkish	**curry** Tamil	**mesa** Latin
omelet Latin	**sierra** Latin	**soy** Mandarin Chinese
squirrel Greek	**tortilla** Late Latin	

Part One

INTRODUCTION TO LETTER PATTERNS

CHAPTER ONE

Letter Patterns

SPELLING IN ENGLISH

This section will get you warmed up for the kind of work you'll be doing in the rest of the book. It is based on the idea that there is a relationship between what you see when you look at a word written down, and what you hear when a word is spoken aloud. Because this relationship is not always clear, sometimes you have to analyze a word to understand it.

What IS correct spelling?

People are fond of pointing out that even Shakespeare, that great master of the written word, was known to spell his own last name in different ways at different times. In fact, the goal of having a single correct spelling for a word is a fairly new idea. For years and years, nobody thought that spelling the same word in different ways was such a problem. Spelling of English started to become regular in the 1600s–1700s.

And would you believe that after several hundred years of trying to regularize our spelling, we still haven't managed? In the 1970s—not that long ago in the history of English—Lee C. Deighton compared four of the major American English dictionaries and found considerable disagreement about the "right" way to spell several thousand common English words. Not only do the dictionaries all offer multiple correct spellings, but they often disagree with each other about how to spell the words.

Here are some examples. How do you spell the word we usually say when we part company? Well, according to Deighton's study, it could be *good-by, goodby, good-bye,* or *goodbye.* If you're scared, you might be *chickenhearted,* or you might be *chicken-hearted.* That healthy stuff you ate for lunch might be *yogurt, yoghurt,* or *yoghourt.* And a song that is traditionally sung to a newly married couple takes the cake! It can be spelled *shivaree, charivaree, chivaree, chivari,* or *charivari.* Is that confusing, or what?

BRAIN TICKLERS
Set # 3

1. Here are some words that have more than one "correct" spelling in English. Using a dictionary at home, in the library or at school, or on the Internet, find at least one alternate spelling for each word. Record your findings. Hint: The spellings below are from the *American Heritage* dictionary, so you might want to try using a different one.

clear-headed	per cent	teen-age
corn flakes	retrorocket	

2. How many different spellings can you find for the word *boogieman*? Write down the names of the dictionaries you used and the spellings you found.

(Answers are on page 29.)

Nobody is ever finished learning to spell

It's important to realize that learning to spell is a process that isn't complete for anyone. As you've seen, we can't agree on how to spell a large number of words correctly. And in addition, we're constantly adding new words to English—people create concepts and invent equipment with new names, and slang terms and phrases arise. Besides that, as we learn new subject areas and skills, we need a new vocabulary so we can talk about our experience.

It's true that some people have an easier time spelling than others. But spelling is something that everyone has to pay attention to. So now let's look at the way we learn to spell.

We start with sound

Think about how people learn language. Maybe you have a younger brother or sister, or maybe a baby lives next door to you. Do they start off learning English by trying to write words? Of course not! They listen to people speak English, and they begin by learning that the sounds they hear can be understood as words, each of which MEANS something. To them, *dog* is a group of sounds that refers to a furry, four-legged beast that licks their faces.

And that's the key to thinking about words—words are sounds written down. After you figure this out—after you understand that written words are a code for the sounds of words spoken aloud—you can learn to read and write. And eventually you get to the point at which you realize that if you want to be understood easily, you have to write d-o-g, and not d-a-w-g or d-a-u-g.

But this is where English can get confusing. Because if you want to write the word *saw*, you spell the same sound that you hear in the middle of *dog* but with the letters *a-w;* and if you want to write the word *sauce*, you spell it *a-u*. The job of this book is to help you figure out the different ways to spell the sounds you hear by giving you rules and strategies. Then you can understand and remember the different patterns for recording the sounds of English. And the most important tool for making sound patterns in writing is, of course, the alphabet.

The alphabet

Okay. We've got the English alphabet with 26 letters. And each letter, by itself, can represent one or more sounds. (For example, you probably know by now that the vowels can have a long or short pronunciation and that the letter *c* can be pronounced like the letter *k* or like the letter *s*, depending on the context.)

But when you put letters together, you can record some sounds that you can't record with a single letter, AND you can duplicate some sounds that you could already make with one letter. (For example, the letters *ow* spell a sound that you can't spell with one letter, but *ph* can indicate the same sound as *f* does by itself.)

And when you put some letters next to others, the sound changes. (For example, an *r* following a vowel can change the pronunciation of the vowel.)

This sounds really complicated. And some people get really upset about it. The British playwright George Bernard Shaw scoffed that you could just as well spell *fish* as *ghoti* if you used *gh* from *rough*, *o* from *women*, and *ti* from *nation*. The problem of spelling was so important to Shaw, that when he died, he left A LOT of his money for the purpose of trying to reform English spelling so it would have one, and only one, symbol for each sound. But it didn't happen.

BRAIN TICKLERS
Set # 4

Make up a new spelling of a word the same way George Bernard Shaw did. Share it with a classmate or friend, and see if he or she can figure out what word you spelled.

(Answers are on page 29.)

The patterns

As we've already pointed out, some sounds can be spelled in more than one way. This makes English more complicated than, say, Spanish, in which each letter has just one pronunciation (on the whole). But there IS a limit. Some people would rather not know about the complications. But my approach to difficulties is to examine them to see what you've got: Once you know where you stand, you can plunge in and try to come to terms with whatever it is. So that's what I'm going to try to help you do.

BRAIN TICKLERS
Set #5

Read each word aloud. Listen to the sound represented by the bold letter(s). Try to think of other words in which the same sound is spelled in a different way. Write down all the words you think of—the more the better. DON'T LOOK AHEAD AT THE CHART UNLESS YOU'RE REALLY, REALLY STUCK.

1. m**a**d
2. b**i**t
3. m**e**
4. n**o**
5. lea**f**
6. **sh**oe
7. **t**iger

(Answers are on page 29.)

Some helpful words

We will have an easier time talking and thinking about spelling if we have some vocabulary to name some special spelling concepts.

// Slash marks are used to set off symbols that we use to show sounds. The slash marks let you know that they're not letters or words:

a is a word, the English indefinite article; we use italics to show words and letters.

/ă/ is the vowel sound in the first syllable of the word *Batman*.

The dictionary used for sounds, symbols, meaning, and pronunciation in this book is *The American Heritage Dictionary of the English Language*. The symbols used in this book for the sounds of words are the symbols used in the first entry of a word in *The American Heritage Dictionary of the English Language*.

Sometimes there is more than one correct way to spell or pronounce a word. Why? Well, there are a few reasons.

1. The spelling of some words has changed over time. For example, *town* used to be spelled with an *e* on the end—*towne*.

2. American and British spelling have become differentiated. The British commonly:

    use a double *l* where we use a single *l* (*traveller* vs. *traveler*),

    use *ou* in cases where we use just an *o* (*colour* vs. *color*),

    use an *re* ending where we use an *er* ending (*theatre* vs. *theater*),

    use a *ce* ending where we use an *se* ending (*defence* vs. *defense*), and keep an *e* between syllables where we drop it (*judgement* vs. *judgment*).

3. There are some spellings that have become acceptable in advertising and brand names:

   doughnut has become *donut*
   light has become *lite*
   night has become *nite*
   school has become *skool*

4. Some foreign words have entered our language through multiple avenues and so continue to have multiple spellings. Remember *shivaree* (p. 6)? It comes to us through French.

If a word has multiple pronunciations or spellings that are acceptable, the dictionary will have multiple entries for it. The first entry is preferred, but all of the entries are correct and accurate English.

blend A consonant blend has two distinct sounds that follow one after the other.
Some blends are written with two consonant letters (for example, *st*) and some have three letters (for example, *str*). All blends have either an *l* (as in *bl*), an *m* (as in *mp*), an *n* (as in *sn*), an *r* (as in *gr*), an *s* (as in *sp*), or a *w* (as in *tw*). Some blends have more than one of these letters.

consonant/vowel Consonants and vowels are sounds, not letters. There are consonant letters (*k*, *l*, *m*, *n*, *x*) and vowel letters (*a*, *e*, *i*, *o*, *u*, and *y*). Sometimes the letters we call consonant letters are used as auxiliary letters in spelling a vowel. For example,

GH helps spell the long *i* sound in the word *sigh*.

W helps spell the vowel sound /ow/ in the word *cow*.

Some consonant sounds are spelled using "vowel" letters.

U spells the /w/ sound in the word *quick*.

Y can represent either a vowel sound, as in *happ*y, or a consonant sound, as in *yes*.

digraph A digraph is literally a string of two letters that may be vowel letters or consonant letters—*di*- means "two" and *graph* means "letter." We're going to use it in a specialized meaning to refer to a group of two or three consonant letters that represent a new sound different from the sounds represented by any of the individual consonant letters by itself.

Examples of consonant letter digraphs are
shoe /sh/
church /ch/ and
thirst /th/.

diphthong A diphthong is a vowel sound with a change during its production. If you say VERY slowly the words *brown*, *bite*, and *boy*, you will probably hear the change at the same time as you feel your mouth move. Each of those words has a vowel diphthong.

phoneme A phoneme is a single sound. A particular phoneme may have one or more spellings.

pronunciation Although some pronunciations of words are simply "wrong," there is often more than one correct way to say a word. This is because pronunciation of English varies. A teacher may be able to help you identify which differences are because of dialect (the version of English you speak) and which might be caused by mispronunciation.

How do you spell . . . ?

The charts on the following pages will show you the range of possibilities for spelling some of the main sounds of English. You'll see some patterns that you found when you did Brain Ticklers Set # 5, and maybe you'll also see some you didn't think of. You DON'T have to memorize them. You might want to put a sticky note on the first page so you can find it again.

Caution—Major Mistake Territory!

Since people pronounce words differently, some of the words in the chart may appear to you to be in the wrong place. (An * will call your attention to some of these words.) Don't worry about it now.

Note: In the chart, an underline _ stands for a consonant letter. So, for example, a_e could represent *ate*, *ace*, *age*, or *ape*. In addition, the letter combinations can appear at the beginning, middle, or the end of a word, or be an entire word in themselves. For example, *a _ e* could be:

N*ate*	(end)
ace	(whole word)
*age*nt	(beginning)
dr*ape*r	(middle)

Common means that these are the most frequently occurring spellings of this sound.

Unusual means that these spellings are less frequent.

Oddball means that these spellings are very rare and may even be unique.

SOUND	SPELLINGS		
	Common	Unusual	Oddball
short *a* /ă/	*a* as in *bat*	*a__e* as in *trance* *al* as in *half** *au* as in *laugh** *i* as in *meringue*	*a_e* as in *comrade*
short *e* /ě/	*e* as in *bet* *ea* as in *bread*	*a* as in *any* *ai* as in *said* *ei* as in *leisure** *eo* as in *leopard* *u* as in *bury* *ue* as in *guess*	*ie* as in *friend*
short *i* /ĭ/	*e* as in *English* *i* as in *bit*	*a_e* as in *advantage* *ia* as in *carriage* *u* as in *busy* *y* as in *abyss*	*ie_e* as in *sieve* *o* as in *women* *ui* as in *build*
short *u* /ŭ/ in an accented syllable	*o* as in *oven* *u* as in *but*	*oo* as in *flood* *ou* as in *trouble*	*oe* as in *doesn't*

SOUND	SPELLINGS		
	Common	Unusual	Oddball
schwa /ə/ in an unaccented syllable	*a* as in *balloon* *e* as in *celebrate* *o* as in *prison* *u* as in *circus*	*ai* as in *captain* *eo* as in *dungeon* *i* as in *pencil* *ia* as in *special* *iou* as in *anxious* *ou* as in *generous*	
long *a* /ā/	*a* as in *favor* *a_e* as in *male* *a__e* as in *paste* *ai* as in *mail* *ai_e* as in *praise* *ay* as in *may*	*ae* as in *Gaelic* *é* as in *soufflé* *e_e* as in *crepe** *ea* as in *great* *ee* as in *matinee* *ei* as in *veil* *eigh* as in *neighbor* *et* as in *bouquet* *ey* as in *prey*	*aigh* as in *straight* *au* as in *gauge*
long *e* /ē/	*e* as in *me* *e_e* as in *genes* *ea* as in *peal* *ee* as in *peek* *y* as in *happy*	*ae* as in *archaeology* *ay* as in *quay* *ea_e* as in *peace* *ei* as in *receive* *ie* as in *thief* *ey* as in *key* *i* as in *curious* *i_e* as in *machine* *is* as in *chassis* *oe* as in *subpoena*	*eo* as in *people*
long *i* /ī/	*i* as in *mild* *i_e* as in *mile* *ie* as in *lie* *igh* as in *might* *y* as in *my*	*ai* as in *Thailand* *ay* as in *papaya* *ei* as in *stein* *eigh* as in *height* *ey* as in *eye* *is* as in *island* *ye* as in *bye* *y_e* as in *rhyme*	*ais* as in *aisle* *oy* as in *coyote* *ui_e* as in *guide*

SOUND	SPELLINGS		
	Common	Unusual	Oddball
long o /ō/	o as in no o_e as in mole oa as in moat oe as in doe ow as in mow	au as in chauvinist eau as in plateau oh as in oh ol as in folk ou as in soul ough as in though	eo as in yeoman ew as in sew owe as in owes
long u /o͞o/	ew as in stew o as in to oo as in soon o_e as in whose u as in Ruth u_e as in June	eu as in sleuth oe as in canoe ou as in you ue as in Sue ui as in suit	ough as in through wo as in two
long u with y in front /yo͞o/	ew as in ewe u as in human u_e as in mule	eu as in feud iew as in view ue as in barbecue	eau as in beauty
/oi/	oi as in boil oy as in boy		uoy as in buoy
/ou/	ou as in cloud ow as in frown	hou as in hour ough as in bough	
/ôr/	ar as in quarrel or as in condor ore as in galore	aur as in centaur oar as in roar oor as in door our as in four	
/ûr/	ear as in learn er as in kernel ir as in bird or as in work ur as in burn	ere as in were eur as in entrepreneur irr as in whirr our as in courtesy urr as in burr	olo as in colonel yrrh as in myrrh
/îr/	ear as in dear eer as in deer er as in zero ere as in here	eir as in weird ier as in tier	eor as in theory

SOUND	SPELLINGS		
	Common	**Unusual**	**Oddball**
/âr/	*air* as in *lair*	*aer* as in *aerobic*	*ayer* as in *prayer* (not the person, who's a /prā´ər/)
	ar as in *parent*	*aire* as in *millionaire*	*eir* as in *heir*
	are as in *snare* *ear* as in *pear*	*er* as in *scherzo*	
/ch/	*ch* as in *chimp* *tch* as in *watch*	*c(e)* as in *cello* *t(e)* as in *righteous* *t(i)* as in *question* *t(ure)* as in *creature*	
/j/	*dg(e)* as in *judge* *g(e)* as in *gentle* *j* as in *jump*	*g(i)* as in *giraffe*	*d(i)* as in *soldier*
/f/	*f* as in *leaf* *ph* as in *photo*	*ff* as in *difficult* *gh* as in *tough* *lf* as in *calf*	
/k/	*c* as in *camel* *ck* as in *back* *k* as in *kangaroo* *q(u)* as in *conquer*	*cc* as in *accurate* *ch* as in *ache* *que* as in *oblique*	*kk* as in *trekked*
/n/	*n* as in *pin* *nn* as in *inn*	*gn* as in *gnat* *kn* as in *knee* *pn* as in *pneumonia*	*dne* as in *Wednesday*
/r/	*r* as in *rare*	*rh* as in *rhythm* *rr* as in *terror* *wr* as in *wring*	*rt* as in *mortgage*

SOUND	SPELLINGS		
	Common	**Unusual**	**Oddball**
/s/	*c(e/i/y)* as in *slice* *s* as in *slime* *ss* as in *brass*	*ps* as in *pseudonym* *sc* as in *science* *st* as in *listen* *sw* as in *sword* *z* as in *quartz*	
/sh/	*c(i)* as in *suspicion* *sh* as in *shoe* *ss(i)* as in *mission* *t(i)* as in *gumption*	*c(e)* as in *oceanic* *ch* as in *chandelier* *s(u)* as in *sugar* *sch* as in *schism* *sc(i)* as in *conscience* *s(e)* as in *nauseous* *ss(u)* as in *tissue*	*chs* as in *fuchsia* *psh* as in *pshaw*
/t/	*t* as in *tiger* *tt* as in *cattle*	*bt* as in *debt* *ed* as in *vanished* *pt* as in *pterodactyl* *th* as in *thyme*	*cht* as in *yacht* *ct* as in *indict*
/w/	*u* as in *quilt* and *suite* *w* as in *wet* *wh* as in *where*	*(g)u* as in *language* *o* as in *once*	
/z/	*z* as in *zebra*	*s* as in *his* *se* as in *turquoise* *ss* as in *possess* *x* as in *xylophone* *zz* as in *buzz*	
/zh/	*s(i)* as in *decision* *s(u)* as in *unusual*	*g(e)* as in *garage** *z(u)* as in *azure*	*g(i)* as in *regime* *t(i)* as in *equation*

BRAIN TICKLERS
Set # 6

Choose 20 different spellings from the chart. Look up each of the example words in the dictionary to find out what language it came from originally. What conclusions can you draw?

(Answers are on page 30.)

The sound/sight strategy

Here's an overview of one strategy that can help you a lot. Let's call it the **sound/sight strategy** or **SSS**:

1. Look for visual patterns.

2. Look for sound patterns.

3. See how the sound patterns correspond to the visual patterns.

4. See if you can find a rule or rules that explain what's going on.

5. Look for more examples that support the rule.

6. Check your rule or rules for exceptions.

Here's a model for you. Look at this list:

leaf
greed
bread
neat
seed
head

Visually there are two patterns:

EA	**EE**
leaf	greed
bread	seed
neat	
head	

And there are also two sound patterns:

long e	**short e**
leaf	bread
neat	head
greed	
seed	

But it is only by looking at the sound patterns AND the visual patterns together, that we can see what's really going on—three patterns:

Long e		Short e
long e-EA	**long e-EE**	**short e-EA**
leaf	greed	bread
neat	seed	head

BRAIN TICKLERS
Set # 7

Extend the patterns of long and short *e* by adding four words of your own choosing to each of the three categories.

(Answers are on page 30.)

LETTER PATTERNS

Earlier in this chapter, you saw that some sounds in English can be represented by quite a few letters and letter combinations. The chart looked at spelling from a sound point of view. Now, we're going to switch to a visual vantage point and look at the letter combinations to see which different sounds they can spell.

Some letter combinations for vowel sounds

Identical twins

Do you know any sets of identical twins? Have you ever called one of them by the wrong name? Chances are that if you did, you didn't get the answer you expected. Look below, and you'll see a set of identical quintuplets.

1. *i* spells /ă/ in *meringue*

2. *i* spells /ĭ/ in *bit*

3. *i* spells /∂/ in *pencil*

4. *i* spells /ē/ in *curious*

5. *i* spells /ī/ in *mild*

Now, what happens if you call one of them by the name belonging to another of them? In most cases, you just get a strange pronunciation of a word. But if you call *i* No. 2 by *i* No. 1's name, you know what happens? You hear the word *bat* instead of the word *bit*. And if you call *i* No. 2 by *i* No. 3's name, you hear the word *but* instead of the word *bit*. If you call *i* No. 2 by *i* No. 4's name, you hear *beat* or *beet* instead of *bit*. And if you call *i* No. 2 by *i* No. 5's name, you hear *bite* instead of *bit*. Whoops!

BRAIN TICKLERS
Set # 8

Use the chart on pages 15–19. For each letter
or set of letters, write down the different sounds
it can spell. Use the slashes and the symbols
from the chart, plus a sample word. The sample
word can be from the chart, or you can choose
one of your own. If you're not sure, check it in
the dictionary. A sample is given for you.

Letter or Letter Combination	Sound Symbol	Sample Word
a	/ă/	fabulous
a		
e		
i		
o		
u		
y		
ai		
ea		
ei		
ie		
oo		
ou		
ow		
ui		
ear		

(Answers are on page 30.)

BRAIN TICKLERS
Set # 9

There's a saying used in teaching spelling: "When two vowels go walking, the first one does the talking." Analyze the chart you made in Brain Tickler Set # 8. Find examples that support the saying. Find examples that don't support it. What conclusions can you draw?

(Answers are on page 32.)

Some letter combinations for consonant sounds

Party time

Have you ever been in this situation? You want to get together with two or three of your good friends, but they don't know each other, and you're not sure what will happen when they're together. Maybe they'll all try to assert themselves and you'll feel like you're just a bunch of individuals, not a group. Maybe one will do all the talking, and the other will be silent. Or maybe you'll have a wonderful mixture in which every person contributes—a totally new experience. Any of these three things can happen when you combine more than one consonant letter.

Three possibilities

When we put consonant letters together, a variety of things can happen.

1. The consonant letters all keep "talking," and we get a **blend** in which each individual letter's sound can be heard.

Consonant letter combinations that make a blend:

initial: *bl, cl, fl, gl, pl, br, cr, dr, fr, gr, pr, tr, sc, scr, sm, sn, sp, spr, st, str, sw, tw*
final: *ft, ld, lt, mp, nd, nt, sk, st*

2. One of the consonant letters is not heard (a **silent partner**). This can happen either when both consonant letters are the same or when different letters are included in the combination.

Consonant letter combinations with a silent partner:

bb, cc, dd, ff, gg, ll, mm, nn, pp, rr, ss, tt
dg(e), (i)gh, kn, gn, lm, mb, tch

3. The consonant letter combination makes a new sound that neither can make alone (**digraph**).

Consonant letter combinations with a new sound (digraphs):

ch, ph, sh, th (voiced, represented by /th/), *th* (unvoiced), represented by /th/, *wh, ng*

Voiced and *unvoiced* have specialized meanings here. They refer to a distinction in the way a sound is produced. When you say voiced consonants, your vocal chords vibrate. When you say unvoiced consonants, they don't. Put your fingers gently on the front of your throat and say the following pairs of letters, and you'll feel it:

Voiced	Unvoiced
z	s
g	k
v	f
d	t
b	p

Now try saying *the* (voiced) and *thread* (unvoiced). Do you hear and feel the difference?

BRAIN TICKLERS
Set # 10

ch, ph, sh, th (voiced, represented by /th/), *th* (unvoiced, represented by /th/), *wh, ng*

For each of the consonant letter digraphs listed above, write a word that includes it.

(Answers are on page 32.)

BRAIN TICKLERS— THE ANSWERS

Set # 3, page 6

1. Answers will vary depending on the dictionaries and the words chosen. Here is a possible set of responses:

   Merriam Webster's Spellings

clearheaded	percent	teenage
cornflakes	retro-rocket	

2. Answers will vary depending on the dictionary or dictionaries chosen. Here is a possible response:

boogieman	boogeyman	bogeyman
boogyman	bogyman	

Set # 4, page 9

Answers will vary depending on what word you decide to spell and which spelling variants you use. One possible response is:

Oklahoma spelled Auquelliouhoughmmi.
Explanation:

au as in *chauvinist*	**iou** as in *anxious*	**mm** as in *Mommy*
que as in *oblique*	**h** as in *hamburger*	**i** as in *pencil*
ll as in *llama*	**ough** as in *though*	

Set # 5, page 10

The words will vary. Possible responses include:
1. **mad** comrade, salve, laugh
2. **bit** enliven, marriage, business, guilty, gym
3. **me** meal, sneeze, treat, peat, Pete, ski, marine, receive, grieve, silly
4. **no** beau, stole, soap, toe, flow
5. **leaf** thief, scaffold, photograph, trough
6. **shoe** ocean, chamois, vision, mission, nation, sugar
7. **tiger** rattle, Ptolemy, flashed, Thai, debtor, yacht, indict

Set # 6, page 20

Answers will vary. Possible responses include:

azure Persian
bouquet Germanic
buzz Middle English
camel Semitic
chandelier Latin
fuchsia New Latin
garage Frankish

knee Old English
meringue French
pneumonia Greek
rhyme Greek
rhythm Greek
schism Greek
science Latin

slime Old English
soufflé Latin
sword Old English
thyme Greek
women Old English
yacht Middle German

Possible conclusion: From this sampling, the English language seems to have "inherited" many words from Greek, Old English, and Latin, and some (but fewer) from Persian, Frankish, French, Semitic, and Germanic.

Set # 7, page 22

Possible responses:

Long *e* /ē/ spelled EA: heat, beat, seat, treat, sheaf, read (present tense), team, scream, dream, cheat

Long *e* /ē/ spelled EE: greet, feed, speed, need, heed, freed, parakeet, sleet, seem, skeet, creed

Short *e* /ĕ/ spelled EA: thread, tread, dead, read (past tense), lead (the metal), ahead, dread

Set # 8, page 25

Letter or Letter Combination	Sound Symbol	Sample Word
a	/ă/	bat
	/ĕ/	any
	/ĭ/	advantage
	/∂/	balloon
	/ā/	favor
	/ä/	salami
e	/ĭ/	English
	/∂/	celebrate
	/ē/	me
i	/ĭ/	bit
	/∂/	pencil
	/ē/	curious
	/ī/	mild

Letter or Letter Combination	Sound Symbol	Sample Word
o	/ĭ/	women
	/ô/	frog
	/ŭ/	done
	/ə/	prison
	/ō/	no
	/o͞o/	who
u	/ĕ/	bury
	/ĭ/	busy
	/ŭ/	but
	/ə/	hubbub
	/o͞o/	Ruth
	/yo͞o/	human
y	/ĭ/	abyss
	/ē/	happy
	/ī/	my
ai	/ĕ/	said
	/ə/	captain
	/ā/	mail
	/ī/	Thailand
ea	/ĕ/	bread
	/ā/	great
	/ē/	peal
ei	/ĕ/	leisure
	/ā/	veil
	/ē/	receive
ie	/ē/	thief
	/ī/	lie
oo	/ŭ/	flood
	/o͞o/	soon
ou	/ŭ/	trouble
	/ə/	generous
	/o͞o/	you
	/ou/	cloud
ow	/ō/	mow
	/ŏ/	knowledge
	/ou/	frown
ui	/ĭ/	build
	/o͞o/	suit

Letter or Letter Combination	Sound Symbol	Sample Word
ear	/ä/	heart
	/â/	pear
	/ûr/	learn
	/îr/	dear

Set # 9, page 26

It's true when *ai* spells /ā/; when *ea* spells /ĕ/ or /ē/; when *ei* spells /ē/; when *ie* spells /ī/; when *ow* spells /ō/; and when *ui* spells /o͞o/. In all other cases it is not true. You may conclude that it has limited use and that it might be more confusing than helpful.

Set # 10, page 28

Answers will vary. Possible responses:

Consonant letter combinations that make a blend:
initial

blossom	**cl**ean	**fl**ood	**gl**ade
plaid	**br**eakfast	**cr**eep	**dr**agon
frontier	**gr**anola	**pr**une	**tr**igonometry
scamp	**scr**eam	**sm**elly	**sn**are **dr**um
spit	**spr**ing	**st**atue	**str**eam
swift	**tw**ilight		

final

le**ft**	shie**ld**	ha**lt**	dam**p**
ki**nd**	de**nt**	ta**sk**	la**st**

Consonant letter combinations with a silent partner:

ba**bb**le	ra**cc**oon	wa**dd**le	gira**ff**e
gi**gg**le	wa**ll**	ha**mm**er	Da**nn**y
ha**pp**y	fe**rr**y	hi**ss**	ca**tt**le
ju**dg**e	**n**ight	**kn**ee	**gn**aw
ca**lm**	la**mb**	la**tch**	

Consonant letter combinations with a new sound (digraphs):

charm	**ph**oto	si**ng**	**wh**ale
thumb (unvoiced)	**sh**eep	**th**at (voiced)	

(Did you know that technically speaking, the letters *wh* starting a word should be pronounced /hw/? In fact, some words that begin w-h used to begin h-w! *Whelp* used to be *hwelp*. *While* used to be *hwil*. Hwat do you think of that?)

CHAPTER TWO

"Let's Start at the Very Beginning"

THREE-LETTER WORDS: "A VERY GOOD PLACE TO START"

Do you remember kindergarten and first grade? Often in early schooling, simple facts in mathematics and spelling are taught with the idea of family. There are number families like 2, 5, and 7, that you can put together in addition and subtraction problems. There are word families, too.

To begin with, there are some really big patterns that we can call *dynasties*. These are identified by the patterns of consonant and vowel letters that they contain. To show them, we use a capital *V* to represent a vowel letter and a capital *C* to represent a consonant letter.

In the area of three-letter words, we can find CCV words like *pry*, and VCC words like *ohm*. There are CVV words like *goo*, VVC words like *aah*, and VCV words like *axe*. Just for review, we're going to spend a little time with three-letter word families that fit the pattern: consonant letter-vowel letter-consonant letter (CVC).

The kiddle in the middle

Having just three letters in a CVC dynasty word narrows the possibilities of letter combinations. But wait! Can you think of ANY three letter CVC words that have a *y* in the middle? No? Well, there are at least two words—*gyp* and *gym*— but the possibilities just got even fewer. There just aren't that many things you can do with only three letters. But what you CAN do is worth exploring.

Group 1—The rhyming group

First, let's define one group of three-letter words and then hunt for families that fit.

> Three-letter-word Group 1 is a collection of three-letter words that have the same middle letter and the same final letter. Most of the words in each family of this group rhyme with each other.

An example of a family in this group is: *bun, fun, gun, Hun* (as in Attila), *nun, pun, run, sun.*

Notice how the list goes in alphabetical order? The easiest way to find members of the family is to go through the alphabet and try each letter on the front of the word to see if it fits. Also notice that proper nouns are allowed into the family. So are weird words. If you're doing the *it* family, you can include *zit.* Is there a family for *ez?* You bet. *Pez* (those little candies) and *fez* (a felt hat worn in eastern Mediterranean countries) will make a family for *ez*, if anyone asks you. The only rule is, if you're working with others, don't include any words that would offend them or show disrespect.

Can you think of any two three-letter words that have the same two last letters, but do NOT rhyme? How about *cut* and *put?*

BRAIN TICKLERS
Set # 11

So who has the biggest family in Group 1? I'll give you a hint: families like *ez* are minuscule (really small) compared with some families you can find. So here's a challenge. What's the biggest family you can find in Group 1? On your mark, get set, go! Hint: If you aren't sure if the letters you've put together make a word, check the biggest dictionary you can find. (The bigger the dictionary, the more words are in it—and yours might be there, too!)

(Answers are on page 50.)

Group 2—New beginnings

Are you ready for the next group? This group of words all begin with the same letters, but end with a different letter.

Three-letter-word Group 2 is a collection of three-letter words that have the same initial letter and the same middle letter.

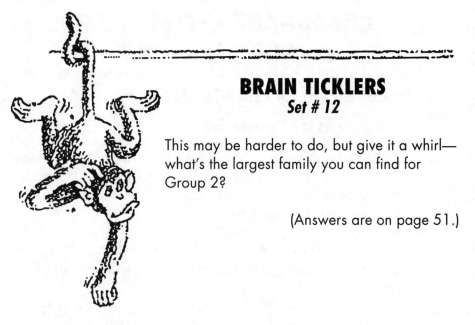

BRAIN TICKLERS
Set # 12

This may be harder to do, but give it a whirl—what's the largest family you can find for Group 2?

(Answers are on page 51.)

Family trees

In all your years of using the English language, you've probably learned some things about English that you don't even realize. See if these conclusions match your experiences in this chapter:

1. The letters x, q, y, c, and z are like distant cousins eight times removed—you hardly ever see them in three-letter words. Can you add other letters to this list?

2. The letter u is like an uncle who lives a few hours away—he appears only when he happens to be in town, less often than a, e, i, and o.

CONSONANT LETTER BLENDS AND DIGRAPHS

Initial digraphs and blends

The musketeers and the molecules

Imagine a CVC word with one or two extra consonant letters in front of it. Now you've got a CCVC word (or a CCCVC word), and the two (or three) consonant letters in the beginning can fit into two different categories.

1. They can form a **blend,** in which you hear the sound of each, one right after the other, like the first two letters of *blend,* which are the digraph *bl.*

   A blend is like the Three Musketeers: each of them by himself has an identity as a musketeer, and when you put them together, you're still aware of their individual personalities. Try saying these blends to yourself: *st, tw, nd, cr.*

2. Or they can form a **digraph,** which we're using to refer to a group of two or three consonant letters that represents a sound that is not the same as the sound of any of the individual consonant letters alone. Examples are *sh, th, ch.*

   A digraph is like a molecule. When you put oxygen and hydrogen together, you get water, and its properties are different than the properties of either component. By oining things together, you have made something new and different.

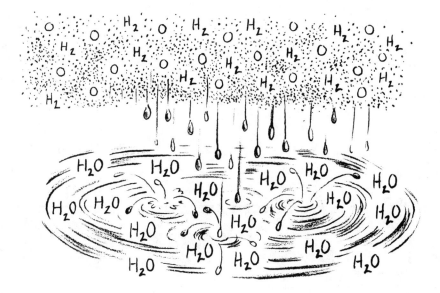

BRAIN TICKLERS
Set # 13

Here is a bunch of initial consonant blends and digraphs. Say them aloud and see if you can tell which are which. Sort them into a group of blends and a group of digraphs.

bl	fl	pr	sm	sw
br	fr	sc	sn	th
ch	gl	sh	sp	tr
cl	gr	scr	spr	tw
cr	ph	sk	st	wh
dr	pl	sl	str	

(Answers are on page 51.)

BRAIN TICKLERS
Set # 14

Okay, now take the same list and sort it into groups that you think are useful. Explain in a sentence or two how you formed your groupings.

bl	fl	pr	sm	sw
br	fr	sc	sn	th
ch	gl	sh	sp	tr
cl	gr	scr	spr	tw
cr	ph	sk	st	wh
dr	pl	sl	str	

(Answers are on page 51.)

BRAIN TICKLERS
Set # 15

Read each list of words below. What do the words in each list have in common? They all are "molecule" words, and they all start with the same digraph. Sort each list into categories that make sense to you. Write a sentence or two explaining why you grouped the items the way you did. Then add three words to each category you made.

1. chalet chameleon Charlotte chauffeur cheese chef chemist cherry chicken chimpanzee choir cholesterol

2. thank-you thaw the then these they thief thistle though thunder

(Answers are on page 52.)

BRAIN TICKLERS
Set # 16

Find some "musketeers": Make a list of five words that begin with each initial consonant letter blend listed below.

bl	*fl*	*pr*	*sm*	*str*
br	*fr*	*sc*	*sn*	*sw*
cl	*gl*	*scr*	*sp*	*tr*
cr	*gr*	*sk*	*spr*	*tw*
dr	*pl*	*sl*	*st*	

(Answers are on page 52.)

BRAIN TICKLERS
Set # 17

Explain the group of initial consonant letters in each of the following words.

thrice   phrase   shrapnel   chrome

(Answers are on page 52.)

Final digraphs and blends

More musketeers and molecules

Imagine a CVC word with one or two extra consonant letters following it. Now you've got a CVCC word (or a CVCCC word), and the two (or three) consonant letters at the end can fit into the same two categories: blends ("musketeers") or digraphs ("molecules").

BRAIN TICKLERS
Set # 18

Take a look at this list of initial blends and digraphs and see if you can figure out which ones can also be final blends and digraphs. Make a list and put down a word for each one that works.

bl	fl	pr	sm	sw
br	fr	sc	sn	th
ch	gl	sh	sp	tr
cl	gr	scr	spr	tw
cr	ph	sk	st	wh
dr	pl	sl	str	

(Answers are on page 53.)

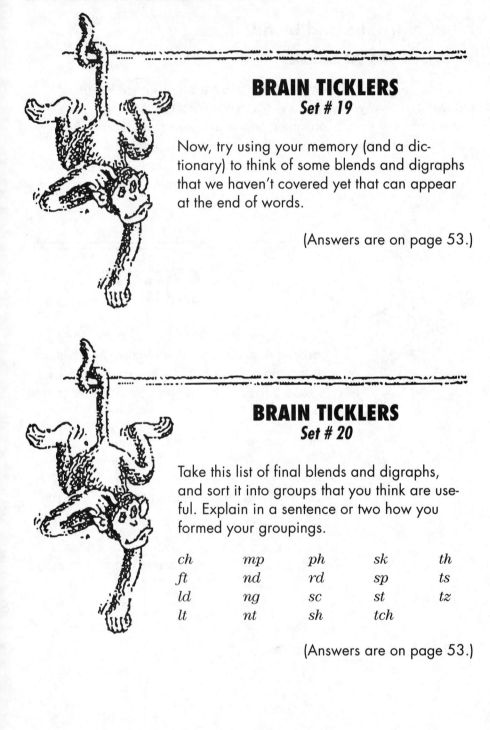

BRAIN TICKLERS
Set # 19

Now, try using your memory (and a dictionary) to think of some blends and digraphs that we haven't covered yet that can appear at the end of words.

(Answers are on page 53.)

BRAIN TICKLERS
Set # 20

Take this list of final blends and digraphs, and sort it into groups that you think are useful. Explain in a sentence or two how you formed your groupings.

ch	mp	ph	sk	th
ft	nd	rd	sp	ts
ld	ng	sc	st	tz
lt	nt	sh	tch	

(Answers are on page 53.)

BRAIN TICKLERS
Set # 21

The digraphs *tch* and *ch* both spell the sound /ch/ at the end of a word. Make a list of as many *tch* and *ch* words as you can think of. What patterns do you find in the middle of your words? Sort the list, not by the final digraph, but by the LETTERS BETWEEN the final digraph and the initial consonant letter, blend, or digraph (if there is one—if not, start with the vowel or two adjacent vowels closest to the final blend or digraph). Write a sentence or two explaining how you grouped the words.

(Answers are on page 53.)

BRAIN TICKLERS
Set # 22

Now, for each final blend and digraph listed below, write five words that contain it.

ft	nd	ph	sk	th
ld	ng	rd	sp	ts
lt	nk	sh	st	tz
mp	nt			

(Answers are on page 53.)

49

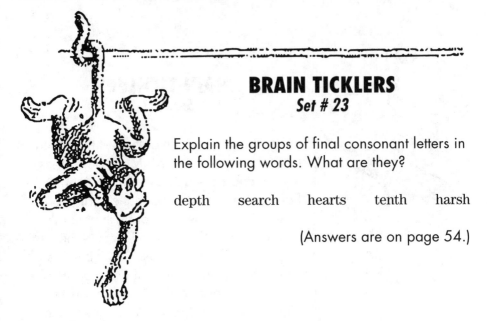

BRAIN TICKLERS
Set # 23

Explain the groups of final consonant letters in the following words. What are they?

depth   search   hearts   tenth   harsh

(Answers are on page 54.)

BRAIN TICKLERS—
THE ANSWERS

Set # 11, page 40

Some of the larger families of Group 1 include:

ED family bed, fed, Jed, led, Ned, red, Ted, wed, zed (another name for the letter *z*) (9)

EW family dew, few, hew, Jew, mew, new, pew, sew, yew (9)

OD family cod, God, hod (holder for coal), mod, nod, pod, rod, sod (grass), Tod (9)

OP family bop, cop, fop, hop, lop, mop, pop, sop, top (9)

UG family bug, dug, hug, jug, lug, mug, pug, rug, tug (9)

AR family bar, car, far, gar (a fish), jar, Lar (a Roman household god), mar, par, tar, war (10)

AT family bat, cat, fat, hat, mat, pat, rat, sat, tat, vat (10)

IN family bin, din, fin, gin, kin, pin, sin, tin, win, yin (Chinese: principle, opposite of yang) (10)

IT family bit, fit, git (British for a worthless person), hit, kit, lit, pit, sit, wit, zit (10)

OG family bog, cog, dog, fog, hog, jog, log, nog (as in eggnog), pog (paper bottlecaps), tog (dress up) (10)

AN family   ban, can, Dan, fan, man, Nan, pan, ran, tan, van, wan (11)
AP family   cap, gap, lap, map, nap, pap, rap, sap, tap, yap, zap (11)
ET family   bet, get, jet, let, met, net, pet, set, vet, wet, yet (11)
OT family   cot, dot, got, hot, jot, lot, not, pot, rot, sot, tot, wot (British verb meaning "know") (12)
AD family   bad, cad, dad, fad, gad, had, lad, mad, pad, rad (a unit of radiation), sad, tad, wad (13)
EN family   Ben, den, fen (low land covered with water), hen, Jen, Ken, men, pen, sen   (an Asian coin), ten, yen, wen (a cyst), Zen (13)
OW family   bow, cow, Dow (Jones average), how, low, mow, now, pow, row, sow, tow, vow, wow, yow (14)

Set # 12, page 41

PE family   ped, peg, pen, pep, per, pet, pew, Pez (8)
SA family   sad, sag, Sam, sap, sat, saw, sax, say (8)
SI family   sic, Sid, sin, sip, sir, Sis, sit, six (8)
SO family   sob, sod, Sol, son, sop, sot, sow, soy (8)
TA family   tab, tad, tag, tan, tap, tar, tat, tax (8)
CA family   cab, cad, Cal, can, cap, car, cat, caw, cay (a coral reef) (9)
MA family   Mac, mad, man, map, mar, mat, maw, Max, may (9)
PA family   pad, pal, Pam, pan, par, pat, paw, pax, pay (9)
WA family   Wac (Women's Army Corps), wad, Waf (Women in the Air Force), wag, war, was, wax, way (8)
RA family   rad (dose of radiation), rag, rah, Raj (British rule in India), ram, ran, rap, rat, raw, ray (10)

Set # 13, page 44

Blends: *bl br cl cr dr fl fr gl gr pl pr sc scr sk sl sm sn sp spr st str sw tr tw*
Digraphs: *ch ph sh th wh*

Set # 14, page 44

Answers may vary. Possible responses follow:
three-letter blends: *scr, spr, str*
blends with a /k/ sound: *cl, cr, sc, scr, sk*
l-blends: *bl, cl, fl, gl, pl, sl*
p-blends: *pl, pr, spr*
r-blends: *br, cr, dr, fr, gr, pr, scr, spr, str, tr*
s-blends: *sc, scr, sk, sl, sm, sn, sp, spr, st, str, sw*
t-blends: *st, str, tr, tw*
digraphs: *ch, ph, sh, th, wh*
digraphs that can have more than one sound: *ch, th*

Set # 15, page 45

Possible responses:

1. **ch sounds like /k/:** chameleon, chemist, choir, cholesterol
   ch sounds /sh/: chalet, Charlotte, chauffeur, chef
   ch sounds like /ch/: cheese, cherry, chicken, chimpanzee

   Additional words:
   ch sounds like /k/: choreography, cholera, chasm, chameleon, charisma
   ch sounds /sh/: Cheyenne, chateau, chaparral, chanticleer, chaise lounge
   ch sounds like /ch/: chess, cheddar, Chinese, chapter, chinchilla

2. **th sounds like /th/:** thank-you, thaw, thief, thistle, thunder
   th sounds like /*th*/: the, then, these, they, though

   Additional words:
   th sound like /th/: thick, thermometer, thrill, thesaurus, theater
   th sounds like /*th*/: thy, that, themselves, there, they'd

Set # 16, page 46

Answers will vary. Possible answers include:

bl	blond, blood, blimp, bloated, black
br	brown, brawny, bruised, brooding, Brahman
cl	clown, closet, cloister, cloudy, clunk
cr	crumpet, cruise, crooked, crocodile, Creole
dr	drip, drum, dreadful, dromedary, droll
fl	Florida, flippers, floral, flea, flowing
fr	Frisbee, fry, fraud, frazzled, frosting
gl	gloat, glad, glutton, gloaming, glacier
gr	green, grab, gruesome, grueling, gravel
pl	plunk, plank, plink, plumber, plywood
pr	predator, prune, prominent, pragmatic, prairie dog
sc	scattered, scapegoat, scuttle, scab, scone
scr	scram, scream, scrap, scrape, scrimshaw
sk	skunk, skim, skillet, skeleton, ski
sl	slam, slang, slippery, slap, sloop
sm	smash, smithereens, smuggle, smelly, smorgasbord
sn	sneeze, snort, snicker, sneer, snigger
sp	spell, spittoon, spawn, spangled, spider
spr	spring, sprightly, spruce, sprinkles, spray
st	stab, stirrup, stellar, staring, steal
str	stream, stripe, strobe, strum, strong
sw	swipe, sweet, swell, swagger, swing
tr	trivia, treehouse, trapper, triangular, tragedy
tw	twerp, tweet, twister, twirl, tweak

Set # 17, page 46

They are all blends composed of a digraph and *r*.

Set # 18, page 47

ch peach	**sh** shush	**st** forest
ph telegraph	**sk** disk	**th** forsooth
sc disc	**sp** grasp	

Set # 19, page 48

Possible answers:

ft	lt	nd	nt	tch
ld	mp	ng	rd	ts

Set # 20, page 48

Possible responses:

two blends or digraphs that make the same sound: sc/sk tch/ch tz/ts
digraph that makes two different sounds: ch
t blends: ft lt nt st ts tz
s blends: sc sk sp st ts
digraphs: ch ng ph sh tch th

Set # 21, page 49

Possible responses:

ch words with Vr: torch, perch, arch, birch, lurch
ch words with Vn: conch, bench, pinch, ranch, scrunch
ch words with V: rich, much, loch, attach
ch words with VV: pouch, peach, pooch, poach, screech
ch words with VVC: haunch, search
tch words with V: watch, witch, etch, Dutch, Scotch

Set # 22, page 49

ft	theft, raft, drift, aloft, tuft
ld	scald, held, gild, bold, guild
lt	halt, pelt, gilt, bolt, guilt
mp	damp, hemp, limp, chomp, bump
nd	wand, wend, wind, bond, cummerbund
ng	tang, zing, gong, lung, sling
nk	yank, fink, plonk, skunk, oink

nt   rant, accent, flint, don't, blunt
ph   graph, aleph, hieroglyph, humph, triumph
rd   weird, beard, bird, cord, curd
sh   ash, mesh, wish, gosh, blush
sk   mask, desk, risk, kiosk, rusk
sp   clasp, wisp, cusp, hasp, grasp
st   fast, fest, fist, cyst, dust
th   bath, Elizabeth, pith, sooth, truth
ts   gnats, bets, kits, plots, guts
tz   ersatz, klutz

Set #23, page 50

depth   blend of *p* and digraph *th*
search   blend of *r* and digraph *ch*
hearts   blend of *r, t,* and *s*
tenth   blend of n and digraph *th*
harsh   blend of r and digraph *sh*

CHAPTER THREE

Vowel Sounds

SHORT VOWEL SOUNDS

A vowel is not what you think

The vowels in English are *a, e, i, o, u,* and sometimes *y,* right? Wrong! Remember, a vowel is not a letter—it's a sound during which air flows from your throat through and out of your mouth without being stopped. If the air is partially or completely cut off during a sound, then you've made a consonant sound.

The letters named above USUALLY represent vowel sounds. But there are exceptions. Sometimes letters we have come to think of as "vowels" may represent consonant sounds. For example, the letter *u* often represents the consonant sound /w/, as in the word *quiet.* And sometimes the letters we think of as consonants help to represent vowel sounds, as in the word *delight,* where the letters *i, g,* and *h* work together to display a vowel sound /ī/.

We classify English vowel sounds into groups to make it easier to think and talk about them. Common groupings include: **short, long, r-controlled,** and **diphthongs.** We are going to talk about each of these groups in separate sections to help you focus.

Diphthongs!?

Introducing . . . (drumroll) the shorts

The letters *a, e, i, o,* and *u* each have a "short" form (short because they sound for a shorter time, so it's said). They are heard in the following words:

a cat   **e** bedbug   **i** iguana   **o** grasshopper   **u** butterfly

Wait! Stop! Hold everything! Let's rewind to *grasshopper*. The sound of the *o* in *grasshopper* is a PROBLEM AREA in English. Why? Try this experiment.

BRAIN TICKLERS
Set # 24

all awful bah bazaar bore bought
call caught caw chalk cod collar
cot daughter father frog gnaw
guard guitar heart honor horse
knowledge laundry lot pot quality
salami sauce sergeant stalk taut
tot wharf

1. Say all of these words out loud to yourself. Make lists (as many as you need) to show the different vowel pronunciations you use when you say the bold-faced letters. Note: There is no right or wrong answer. Just divide the words into the categories YOU use.

2. Now look at the answers from *The American Heritage Dictionary of the English Language*. Compare and contrast your groups with the dictionary's groups. What observations can you make? Now compare your answers with the *Merriam Webster's* groupings.

3. Now classify each of your groups according to the spellings of the vowel sound. Briefly explain your classifications.

(Answers are on page 74.)

Dia-who?

People in different parts of America (and elsewhere) who speak English pronounce words somewhat differently, depending on the regional **dialect** that they speak. A dialect is a subset of a language, usually confined to a particular region. There are three main dialect areas in the United States: Northern, Southern, and Midland. But the differences in pronunciation are so specific, that a language specialist could listen to you and tell whether you are from the Northern Middle West; New England; Chicago; the Central Atlantic Seaboard; Gary, Indiana; the Southern Coast; New York City; and so on. (Black American English is an example of a dialect that is NOT regionalized.) No particular dialect is better than any other dialect, although some may be more popular than others, or people may CLAIM that theirs is superior.

The differences in dialect are noticeable when you listen to the way words like *father* and *hot* are pronounced. In any dictionary you check, you will probably find some words with /ä/ that you pronounce /ŏ/ and vice versa. And dictionaries are by no means in agreement about the number one spelling for these words.

Compared to this, /ă/, /ĕ/, and /ĭ/ are EASY.

BRAIN TICKLERS
Set # 25

For the sounds /ă/, /ĕ/, and /ĭ/, find as many different spellings as you can and write a word that has each spelling. You may use the chart on page 15 for help, but for every spelling you include from the chart, add another word in English that has that spelling.

(Answers are on page 74.)

BRAIN TICKLERS
Set # 26

1. Group the /ă/ spellings you found into categories that make sense to you. Write a sentence or two explaining your categories.

2. Now do the same for /ĕ/.

3. Time to repeat the procedure for /ĭ/.

(Answers are on page 74.)

61

Time out for an explanation

To prepare for talking about short *u*, we need to introduce a couple of terms. Don't worry! You've probably heard these before. The first one is **syllable.** A syllable is a vowel sound, either by itself or with the preceding and following consonant sounds. The word *syllable* has three distinct syllables: syl la ble. How many syllables in *antidisestablishmentarianism?* Twelve (check it out).

All stressed out

Do you know what a **stressed syllable** is? No, it's not one that's had a really hard day. When we say words, we usually say one part more loudly than any other part. That's the primary stress. In the word *metropolis*, we say *trop* louder than the rest. That's the primary stress. In the word *discombobulate* (it means to upset something or mess something up), we say *bob* the loudest, but *dis* and *late*, although softer than *bob*, are louder than *com* and *u*. That's called secondary stress. Try saying it yourself.

One way to represent stress is with little stress flags. Primary stress has a thicker, darker flag than secondary stress.

O ver worked

Uhhhhhhh

When the sound of short *u* appears in a word in a stressed syllable like butterfly, we call it "short *u*." But in a lot of English
words, a sound like short *u* appears in unstressed syllables.
When such a sound appears in an UN-stressed syllable, we call
the sound a **schwa** and represent it with this symbol: ∂.

The word *schwa* comes from a Syriac word meaning "equal"—
maybe because many different sounds are kind of "equalized" into
one sound (more or less) in unstressed syllables. Here are some
examples that will show you how sounds are equalized:

meth**o**dical (short *o*) → meth**o**d (schwa sound)
med**i**cinal (short *i*) → med**i**cine (schwa sound)
tel**e**graphy (short *e*) → tel**e**graph (schwa sound)
tyr**a**nnical (short *a*) → tyr**a**nt (schwa sound)
comb**i**ne (long *i*) → comb**i**nation (schwa sound)

Get the idea?

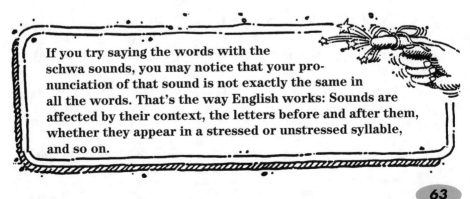

If you try saying the words with the
schwa sounds, you may notice that your pronunciation of that sound is not exactly the same in
all the words. That's the way English works: Sounds are
affected by their context, the letters before and after them,
whether they appear in a stressed or unstressed syllable,
and so on.

BRAIN TICKLERS
Set # 27

Hidden in this word search are the names of nine musical instruments. Three of the instruments have only a short *u* sound. Four of them have only a *∂* sound. Two of them have both a short *u* AND a schwa. Find the words and group them in the proper categories.

```
S  I  U  S  R  I  P  E  C  O  R  O  C  U  P  T  R  M

S  C  R  D  P  E  T  O  C  L  C  R  D  L  E  E  E  A

A  L  M  I  O  R  D  X  X  T  A  O  U  O  T  N  C  D

N  O  I  S  S  U  C  R  E  P  U  L  L  R  U  I  O  O

O  M  R  U  S  O  B  P  O  N  E  T  C  I  N  R  R  U

H  U  U  I  D  D  M  L  I  C  P  O  I  O  M  A  D  B

P  R  A  L  N  U  O  D  E  H  E  X  M  D  I  L  I  C

O  D  C  L  R  M  B  T  O  B  X  R  E  C  C  O  I

S  S  I  T  C  U  E  C  U  S  A  B  R  E  I  R  U  N

S  S  N  T  O  N  C  O  R  H  U  S  E  R  S  X  O  P

X  A  O  D  E  N  O  H  P  O  X  A  S  U  N  E  T  M

A  B  N  I  R  P  H  O  D  D  U  L  C  O  R  I  O  U
```

(Answers are on page 75.)

BRAIN TICKLERS
Set # 28

1. Sort these short vowel words into groups that make sense to you. Write a sentence or two explaining your categories.

   business   calf   dog   dread   necessary
   giraffe   gnat   guest   guild   marriage
   twit

2. Compare these word pairs in which some of the letters are identical. What do you find?

   business/buster
   calf/halt
   dog/ogre
   dread/mead
   necessary/far
   guest/glue
   guild/ennui (This means "boredom"; it's pronounced on-WEE.)

   (Answers are on page 75.)

BRAIN TICKLERS
Set # 29

1. Sort these short *a* words into groups that make sense to you. Write a sentence or two explaining your categories.

   babble   bad   baffle   bag   battle   can
   cattle   haggle   ham   hassle   man
   paddle   rat   stammer   zap

2. Now add short *e*, short *i*, short *o*, and short *u* words to each category you made, if possible.

(Answers are on page 76).

LONG VOWEL SOUNDS

O, i long 4 u

In this section we are going to talk about the sounds called long *a*, *e*, *i*, *o* and *u*. The long vowel sounds are the sounds that you hear when you say the names of the letters *a*, *e*, *i*, *o*, and *u* PLUS the sound /oo/ without the /y/ sound. Even though long *u* has a consonant sound /y/ at the beginning as in the word *cute*, we still call it a vowel sound. As you know, both from your own experience and from the chart in Chapter 2, long vowel sounds are not always spelled with the letter whose name you hear. In fact, some of them have some pretty strange spellings.

Taste your vowels

We usually don't think too much about how vowels feel in our mouths. But if you try these experiments, you'll learn something.

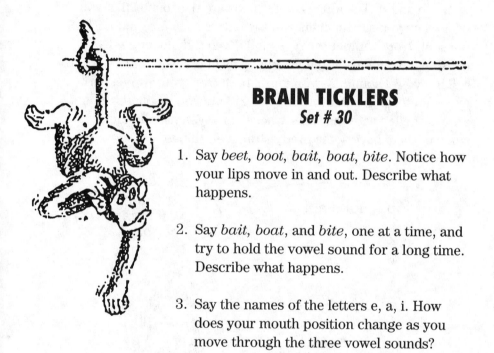

BRAIN TICKLERS
Set # 30

1. Say *beet, boot, bait, boat, bite.* Notice how your lips move in and out. Describe what happens.

2. Say *bait, boat,* and *bite,* one at a time, and try to hold the vowel sound for a long time. Describe what happens.

3. Say the names of the letters e, a, i. How does your mouth position change as you move through the three vowel sounds?

4. Say the short vowels /ă/, /ĕ/, /ĭ/, /ŏ/, /ŭ/. Describe how your mouth changes. Now say the long vowels /ā/, /ē/, /ī/, /ō/, /ū/. Describe how your mouth changes. How were the two sets different?

(Answers are on page 76.)

Now let's see if you can pick out the long vowels by sound (and feel).

BRAIN TICKLERS
Set # 31

Sort this list into words with short vowel sounds and words with long vowel sounds.

bread	seat
flat	flavor
oven	to
he	met
lemonade	comrade
crumb	truth
gauge	laugh
people	leopard
human	but
bit	wild
soon	flood
gym	my
you	trouble

(Answers are on page 76.)

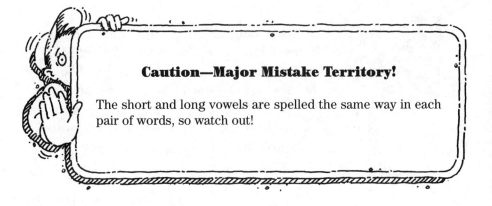

Caution—Major Mistake Territory!

The short and long vowels are spelled the same way in each pair of words, so watch out!

BRAIN TICKLERS
Set # 32

Use the symbols V for vowel letter and C for consonant letter (in combination if necessary) to show patterns of spelling for long vowels /ā/, /ē/, /ī/, /ō/, /yōo/, and /ōo/ that occur in the words in Set # 31. Show the pattern for the entire syllable that the long vowel appears in. Then brainstorm to find other patterns of two to six vowel and consonant letters that can convey long vowel sounds. Next to each pattern you identify, write a word that has the same pattern.

(Answers are on page 77.)

BRAIN TICKLERS
Set # 33

For the sounds of long *a, e, i, o,* and the two forms of long *u,* find as many different spellings as you can and write a word that has that spelling. You may use the chart on pages 16–17 for help, but for every spelling you include from the chart, use a different word in English that has that spelling, if you can find one.

(Answers are on page 77.)

BRAIN TICKLERS
Set # 34

Homophones are words that sound the same but are spelled differently, like *meat* and *meet*. Here is a list of some words with a long vowel sound, each of which has at least one homophone. Write the homophone(s) for each.

1. ale
2. isle
3. bail
4. base
5. Bea
6. beech
7. bow
8. boulder
9. bold
10. breech
11. brake
12. brood
13. bridle
14. buy
15. sealing
16. cheep
17. choose
18. site
19. creek
20. cruise
21. daze
22. due
23. dye
24. dough
25. does (several female deer)

(Answers are on page 79.)

BRAIN TICKLERS
Set # 35

Read the definitions separated by semicolons. Write a set of long vowel homophones that matches each set of definitions.

1. a person who colors cloth; disastrous

2. the overhang at the edge of a roof; the periods between dusk and night

3. the organ of sight; first person singular pronoun; how a sailor says "yes"

4. when a person loses consciousness; a move designed to trick someone

5. destiny; a celebration

6. a small insect that often lives on dogs; to run away

7. lets go from prison; to be very cold; a decorative band around the wall of a room

8. a chicken made especially for cooking in deep fat; a brother in a religious order

9. the pace of a horse; an entrance through a wall

10. to create fine powder out of hard cheese; wonderful and outstanding

(Answers are on page 79.)

BRAIN TICKLERS
Set # 36

How many sets of homophones can you find with different spellings of the same long vowel? (No fair using homophones used in Brain Ticklers Sets # 34 and # 35.)

Get 10 and you're good.
Get 20 and you're an expert.
Get 30 or more and you're out of this world!

(Answers are on page 79.)

BRAIN TICKLERS—
THE ANSWERS

Set # 24, page 59

1. Here are some possible responses based on two dictionaries:

	American Heritage	Merriam Webster's
Group 1	all awful bore bought call caught caw chalk daughter frog gnaw horse laundry sauce stalk taut wharf	all awful bought call caught caw chalk daughter frog gnaw horse laundry sauce stalk taut wharf
Group 2	bah bazaar father guard guitar heart salami sergeant	bore

Group 3	cod collar cot honor knowledge lot pot quality tot	bah bazaar cod collar cot father guard guitar heart honor knowledge lot pot quality salami sergeant tot

2. Answers will vary. You might conclude that pronunciation of these closely related sounds is highly irregular and hard to categorize.

3. Possible response (based on *American Heritage* groupings):
   Most short *o* words are spelled with an *o*, and most are in CVC words.
   /ô/ can be spelled *a, aw, o_e, ough, augh, aw, al, o, au.*
   /ä/ can be spelled *ah, aa, a, a(r), ea(r), e(r).*

Set # 25, page 61

Possible responses:
short a

a rat	*a_ _e* dance	*al* calf
au as in aunt	*i* as in timbre	

short e

a many	*ai* again	*e* debt
ea sweat	*ei* heifer	*eo* jeopardy
u as in burial	*ue* as in guest	

short i

a_e courage	*e* pretty	*i* snit
ia marriage	*u* business	*ui* built
y crystal		

Set # 26, page 61

Possible responses:
1. One-letter spellings: *a, i*
   multiple-letter spellings: *a_e, ai, au*

2. Spellings with *e* in them: *e, ea, ei, eo*
   Spellings without *e* in them: *a, ai, u*

3. Spellings with *i* in them: *i, ia, ui*
   Spellings without *i* in them: *a_e, e, u, y*

Set # 27, page 64

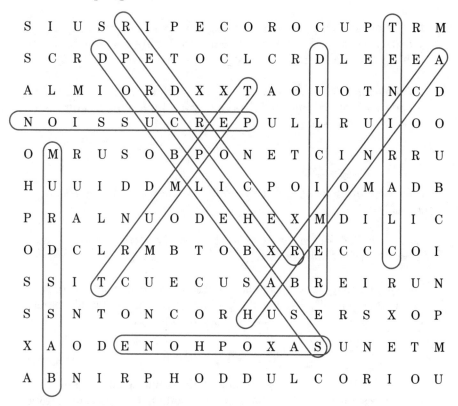

short *u*: trumpet, double bass, bass drum
schwa: harmonica, saxophone, clarinet, recorder
both: percussion, dulcimer

Set # 28, page 65

1. Possible responses:
   short i words: business (spelled *u* and *e*), guild (spelled *ui*), marriage (spelled *ia*), twit (spelled *i*), giraffe (spelled *i*)
   short a words: calf (spelled *al*), gnat (spelled *a*), giraffe (spelled *a_e*)
   short e words: necessary (spelled *e* and *a*), dread (spelled *ea*), guest (spelled *ue*)

2. In each case the identical letters represent different sounds in the two different words.

Set # 29, page 66

1. Possible responses:
   CVC words with short vowels: bad, bag, can, ham, man, rat, zap
   words with short vowels followed by a double consonant: babble, baffle, battle, cattle, haggle, hassle, paddle, stammer

2. **CVC words with short vowels**: fed, lid, cod, mud
   words with short vowels followed by a double consonant: tessellate, hiss, bottle, snuggle

Set # 30, page 68

Your descriptions may be a little different than these, but you'll get the general idea:

1. Lips are pulled back as in a grin for *bee*, *bait*, and *bite*; rounded and forward for *boot* and *boat*.

2. You cannot hold the vowel sound because it's actually made up of two different sounds. The technical term for this (in case you don't remember) is *diphthong*. It may also be called a *vowel glide*.

3. It opens progressively wider for each vowel.

4. Answers will vary. For the short vowels, the sound seems to come from about the same place in the back of my mouth, but my lips and jaw move around to change the vowel. For the long vowels, the sound seems to come from farther forward in my mouth, and just like for the long vowels, my lips and jaw move around to change the vowel. The short vowels and long vowels seem to be in different places in my mouth.

Set # 31, page 69

Short: bread, flat, oven, met, comrade, crumb, laugh, leopard, but, bit, flood, gym, trouble
Long: seat, flavor, to, he, lemonade, truth, gauge, people, human, wild, soon, my, you

Set # 32, page 70

Here are the words from Set # 31:

seat CVVC
flavor CCV
my, to, he CV
lemonade VCV

truth CCVCC
gauge CVVCV
you, people CVV

human CV
wild CVCC
soon CVVC

Here are words and patterns arranged in increasing length (answers will vary):

CV my
VC I'm
CVV jay
CCV cry
VVV eau (it comes from the French word for "water")

CVCC comb
CVVC coat
CVVV beau
CVCe cone
CVCCe waste
CVVCC heist

CVVCe mayonnaise
CVVVC Seoul
CCVCC brush
CCVCCC bright

Set # 33, page 70

Reminder: I have used the term *Oddball* to refer to a rare spelling, maybe even a unique spelling in English. I have not been able to find a definitive list of all possible English spellings for each sound.

Long a

a flavor
a_e tame
a_ _e taste
ae sundae
ai rain
ai_e plaice (It's a fish, and Rudyard Kipling mentions it in the story "How

the Whale Got His Throat.")
aigh ODDBALL
Can you think of anything besides *straight?*
au ODDBALL
Can you think of anything besides *gauge?*

ay bray
é café
e_e fete
ea steak
ee toupee
ei sheik
eigh sleigh
et croquet
ey obey

Long e

ae aegis
ay hurray
e aborigine
e_e athlete
ea pea
ea_e grease
ee employee
ei protein

eo ODDBALL
Can you think of anything besides *people?*
ey monkey
i kiwi
i_e automobile
ie achieve

is ambergris (second pronunciation from *Merriam Webster's Collegiate Dictionary*)
oe Phoebe
y uncanny

VOWEL SOUNDS

Long i

ai naiad and Shanghai—and that's it, according to Edward Carney in *A Survey of English Spelling*

ais Carney says *aisle* is the only English word with this spelling.

ay cayenne (very rare spelling)
ei kaleidoscope
eigh sleight
ey geyser (very rare spelling)
i alibi
i_e crime
ie pie
igh knight
is isle

oy ODDBALL
Can you think of anything besides *coyote*?
ui_e ODDBALL
Can you think of anything besides *guide*?
y wry
ye rye
y_e thyme

Long o

au chauffeur
eau bureau
eo ODDBALL
Can you think of anything besides *yeoman*?
ew ODDBALL
Can you think of anything besides *sew*?
o burro
o_e nose

oa hoax
oe toe
oh Shiloh
ol molt
ou boulder
ough dough
ow bungalow
owe ODDBALL
Can you think of anything besides *owe(s)*?

Note: Here are some other oddball /o/ spellings, just for you:
aoh—pharaoh
eou—Seoul
oo—Roosevelt

Long u /o͞o/

eu rheumatism
ew grew
ho whom
o tomb
oo raccoon
o_e lose
oe shoe (very rare)

ou croup
ough ODDBALL
Can you think of anything besides *through*?
u gnu
u_e prune

ue glue
ui bruise
wo ODDBALL Can you think of anything besides *two*?

Long u /yo͞o/

eau ODDBALL
Can you think of anything besides *beauty*?

ew nephew
iew view
u unity

ue argue
u_e huge

Set # 34, page 71

Possible responses:

1. ail
2. aisle
3. bale
4. bass
5. be, bee
6. beach
7. beau
8. bolder
9. bowled

10. breach
11. break
12. brewed
13. bridal
14. by
15. ceiling
16. cheap
17. chews

18. cite, sight
19. creak
20. crews
21. days
22. dew
23. die
24. doe
25. doze

Set # 35, page 72

1. dyer, dire
2. eaves, eves
3. eye, I, aye
4. faint, feint
5. fate, fete

6. flea, flee
7. frees, freeze, frieze
8. fryer, friar
9. gait, gate
10. grate, great

Set # 36, page 73

1. gale, Gail
2. greys, graze
3. groan, grown
4. grosser, grocer
5. guys, guise
6. heal, heel
7. hew, hue
8. higher, hire
9. hoes, hose
10. knave, nave
11. knead, need
12. knew, new
13. know, no
14. knows, nose
15. liar, lyre
16. load, lode
17. loan, lone
18. made, maid
19. male, mail
20. mane, main
21. maze, maize
22. moat, mote

23. mooed, mood
24. mowed, mode
25. night, knight
26. owed, ode
27. paced, paste
28. pail, pale
29. pain, pane
30. peace, piece
31. peak, peek, pique
32. peal, peel
33. pi, pie
34. plaice, place
35. plane, plain
36. pleas, please
37. pray, prey
38. pried, pride
39. pries, prise, prize
40. pros, prose
41. read, reed
42. road, rode
43. roe, row
44. roes, rows, rose

45. role, roll
46. roomer, rumor
47. rues, ruse
48. sail, sale
49. scene, seen
50. sea, see
51. seam, seem
52. sew, so, sow
53. shone, shown
54. shoot, chute
55. sighed, side
56. sighs, size
57. sign, sine
58. slay, sleigh
59. sleight, slight
60. sold, soled
61. sole, soul, Seoul
62. stake, steak
63. stayed, staid
64. steal, steel
65. stile, style
66. straight, strait
67. suite, sweet
68. swayed, suede
69. tail, tale
70. tea, tee
71. team, teem
72. teas, tease

73. throne, thrown
74. through, threw
75. tied, tide
76. toe, tow
77. towed, toad
78. vain, vane, vein
79. vale, veil
80. wait, weight
81. waste, waist
82. wave, waive
83. way, weigh
84. we've, weave
85. we, wee
86. weak, week
87. weighed, wade
88. whale, wail
89. wheel, weal
90. while, wile
91. whiled, wild
92. whined, wind
93. whole, hole
94. who's, whose
95. wreak, reek
96. wright, write, right, rite
97. wrote, rote
98. yoke, yolk
99. you, ewe, yew

CHAPTER FOUR

Odds and Ends

MISCELLANEOUS VOWEL SOUNDS

R—The control freak

Have you ever heard the term *control freak* for someone who has to dominate the situation? Well, when the letter *r* comes after a vowel, it usually exerts some power over it, changing its sound, so that we call such vowels *r-controlled*, or *r-influenced*, or *rhotic* vowels.

BRAIN TICKLERS
Set # 37

In each pair of words there are the same vowels and the letter that precedes them (if any) is the same. But in one word, the letter *r* follows the vowel(s), and in the other, there is no *r*. Compare each set of words: do they have the same vowel sounds, or different vowel sounds?

fork, fold   park, pack
fur, fun   tore, tone
girl, give   wear, wean
herd, help   work, won't
mirage, mileage

(Answers are on page 101.)

BRAIN TICKLERS
Set # 38

1. Sort the words below into groups that have the same vowel sound.

   sphere   warm   four   wear
   steer   worm   fir   were
   dare   wore   fear   fur
   welfare

2. Add three words of your own choosing to each group you formed.

(Answers are on page 101.)

R u ready for this?

Vowel sounds influenced by the letter *r* following them are shown as wearing little hats. There are four of them: /âr/, /îr/, /ôr/, and /ûr/.

Char has the sound /âr/.
Cheer has the sound /îr/.
Chore has the sound /ôr/.
Chirp has the sound /ûr/.

Caution—Major Mistake Territory!

Other vowel sounds can appear before the letter *r* as well. You can have /or/, /ir/, /ŏor/ (see what follows for more about this sound), and so on. If you don't see a hat on the letter in the pronunciation, then pronounce it in the way indicated: long, short, or what have you.

BRAIN TICKLERS
Set # 39

For the sounds of /âr/, /îr/, /ôr/, and /ûr/ find as many different spellings as you can and write a word that has each spelling. You may use the chart on pages 17–18 for help, but for every spelling you include from the chart, use a different word in English that has that spelling if you can find one.

(Answers are on page 101.)

What's left?

Aren't we done with the vowels yet? Well, not quite. A couple of diphthongs aren't included in the long vowel category, and one sound seems to hang out all by itself. First, the diphthongs:
/oi/ is the vowel sound in the word *boy*.
/ou/ is the vowel sound in the word *ow*.
Easy, huh?
The other guy is a sound that is represented by the symbol /o͝o/, and you hear it in the word *put*.
Now try this sorting exercise.

BRAIN TICKLERS
Set # 40

1. Sort these words into groups according to the sound of the bold letters.

av**oi**d
d**ou**bt
empl**oy**
g**oo**d
Howard
p**ou**t
s**oy**
t**oo**k
w**ou**ld

2. Add three words of your own choosing to each group.

(Answers are on page 102.)

"SILENT" LETTERS

Shhhhhh! Silent letter zone

Some people talk about letters that are not heard making their "usual" sound in a word as *silent*. Other people prefer to talk about these letters in other ways. Edward Carney, author of *A Survey of English Spelling*, distinguishes two kinds of *silent* letters: *auxiliary*, and *dummy*.

Auxiliary letters are part of a group of letters that spell a sound that does not have a usual single letter to represent it. For example:
/th/ thing
/th/ there
/sh/ share
/zh/ treasure
/ng/ song

Dummy letters do not have the same kind of function that auxiliary letters do. There are two different subgroups of dummy letters. **Inert letters** are letters that appear in a word segment every time it occurs, sometimes heard, and sometimes not. For example, the *g* in
resign and resignation, and
malign and malignant
is inert.

That dummy hasn't made a sound.

You can see that the *g* is visually important in recognizing the connection between the words (that is, the word segment is the same in both cases so we know the meanings are related), even though it is pronounced in one instance and not in the other.

Empty letters are letters that seem to do absolutely nothing. They do not have a function like auxiliary letters or inert letters. The letter *u* in the word *gauge* (the only case I can find of *au* = /ā/ in English) is empty. If the word was spelled *gage*, we could read and spell it perfectly well.

Finally, final e

Since we are in a vowel chapter (at least so far), let's start with the most notorious silent letter of them all—silent *e* at the end of a word with a long vowel sound. What's it doing there, anyway? Well, it's there as a marker to tell you that the vowel is long, that's what. **Markers** are letters that do not represent a sound themselves, but that tell us something about the sound of other letters in the word. Final silent *e* is an example of a marker. It signals a long vowel sound in the syllable it finishes. You can tell the difference between

mat and mate
fat and fate
hat and hate
not and note
rot and rote
cut and cute
and so on,
because the *e* is telling you something.

BRAIN TICKLERS
Set # 41

Make ten sets like those above: two one-syllable words, one of which has a short vowel and the other of which has a final e to mark the vowel as long.

(Answers are on page 102.)

A final *e* can also tell you how to pronounce *th* in words like
breath and breathe
cloth and clothe
loath and loathe.
And, conversely, the pronunciation—/th/ or /*th*/—can tell you
whether to spell the word with or without a final *e*.

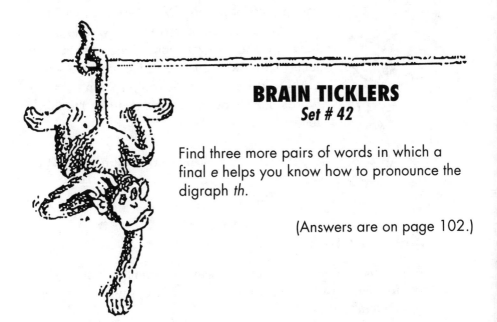

BRAIN TICKLERS
Set # 42

Find three more pairs of words in which a
final *e* helps you know how to pronounce the
digraph *th*.

(Answers are on page 102.)

Double consonants

Well, you may point out, not all long vowels have an *e* to let you
know how to pronounce them. You're right. Another way we
recognize long vowels is that they're not followed by a double
consonant, which often lets us know that the preceding vowel
is short. There are exceptions: *troll* with an /ō/ is one. But many
times, a double consonant at the end of a syllable means the
syllable has a short vowel sound. (There are other reasons for
doubling consonants that will be discussed later when we talk
about endings.)

BRAIN TICKLERS
Set # 43

Make a list of twenty CVCC words in which the double consonant marks the syllable as having a short vowel sound. One rule: the first letter of the two consonants that end the word CANNOT be an r. For example, don't use the words *hurt* or *barn*, which have r as the third letter.

(Answers are on page 103.)

Silent partners

We've looked at some consonants that are "silent" when they help to spell vowel sounds (at least, that's one way to interpret it). Remember these?

She's always helpful but never utters a sound.

eigh spells /ā/ in *neighbor*

is spells /ī/ in *island*

ow spells /ō/ in *mow*

hou spells /ou/ in *hour*

That's one category of silent consonants. But another category is consonants that are silent but unconnected to a vowel sound (usually in a group of two consonants). Here are some examples:

silent *b* comb

silent *h* ghost

silent *k* knight

silent *t* listen

silent *c* scissors

silent *w* wrong

BRAIN TICKLERS
Set # 44

1. How many words can you list that have a silent consonant letter? I have a list of 168 in the answer section (by no means a complete list). Can you find . . . 30? (NO DOUBLE LETTERS e.g., *mm*, *bb*, and so on, ALLOWED IN THIS GAME!!) Hint: letters to focus on: *b, d, g, h, k, p, t, w*

2. Write briefly about any patterns you've found.

(Answers are on page 103.)

HOMOGRAPHS AND HOMOPHONES

Present a present and record a record

Homographs are groups of (usually two) words that are spelled the same way but have different meanings. There are several kinds of homographs.

Related verbs and nouns (like record' and re'cord) with the same spelling but different pronunciations, are not technically homographs because they have the same etymological root, but we're going to include them here because they can present a spelling challenge—you have to remember that even though they sound different, they're spelled the same.

Other related parts of speech can be homographs AND homophones at the same time. When one, for example, has a comparative ending *-er* and the other has the noun suffix *-er,* you get homographs like:

stranger (the person you don't know) and *stranger* (more strange)

cooler (the place you keep things so they don't get warm) and *cooler* (more cool).

BRAIN TICKLERS
Set # 45

For each word in the list below, look in the dictionary to find definitions for two homographs that are NOT homophones. Record the definitions.

1. bass   3. gill   5. real

2. bow   4. lead

(Answers are on page 105.)

BRAIN TICKLERS
Set # 46

Use the clues to help you discover the homographs that will complete the crossword puzzle.

DOWN

1. Several female deer, or the third person singular of a verb meaning "to carry out"

3. Very small, or a duration of time equal to 60 seconds

4. The quality of not being dead, or a verb meaning "to reside in a place"

6. A kind of fish with both eyes on one side of its head, or to thrash about helplessly and without effect

7. Creating a small, bright sound as by hitting a crystal with a pencil, or coloring something slightly

8. Hitting a golf ball a short distance, or the act of placing something in a spot

9. Moving air, or the act of wrapping up something into a ball

ACROSS

2. To start up again, or an organized list of one's activities and employment

5. To strike with sharp blows, or a display of food from which guests may serve themselves

9. Wrapped up string in a ball, or an injury that breaks the skin

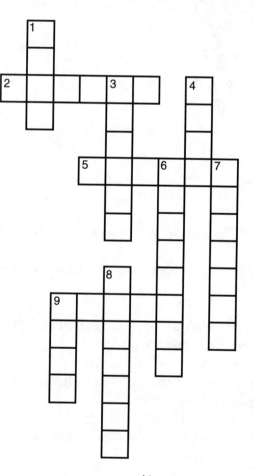

(Answers are on page 106.)

What's /sôs/ for the goose, may be /sŏs/ for the gander

Homophones are groups of (usually two) words that sound the same but are spelled differently. But different people may have different homophones. Why? Because homophones depend on pronunciation, and people with different dialects pronounce words differently. What's a homophone for you may not be a homophone for your best friend.

Hum oh funs

There are several kinds of homophones:

- Single words that come from the same origin, but evolved differently.
- Single words that have different origins.
- A single word or group of words that sounds identical to another group of words, either in English or in another language.

BRAIN TICKLERS
Set # 47

The last group of homophones can be the most fun. An actor and writer, Luis D'Antin Van Rooten, wrote a book called *Mots D'heures: Gousses, Rames* (say it aloud several times—do you get it?), which is filled with little poems. Can you name these in English? Hint: Try saying them aloud.

1. Lit-elle mese moffette

2. Pousse y gâte, pousse y gâte

3. Lille beau pipe

4. Dissolu typique Ouen ou Marquette.

(Answers are on page 106.)

BRAIN TICKLERS
Set # 48

This is a toughy. See if you can invent or create four homophone sets in English. Foreign words are permissible (see below). It's okay if they don't make sense, like:

Don Quixote went to Boston: donkey hoe tea wan tube Austin

(Answers are on page 107.)

Homonyms

When a pair of homographs are also homophones, we call them *homonyms*. Got that? They're word pairs that are spelled the same AND pronounced the same. Examples are
cricket (the game and the insect)
can (the container and the verb that means "to be able")
fine (the penalty and the adjective meaning "good").

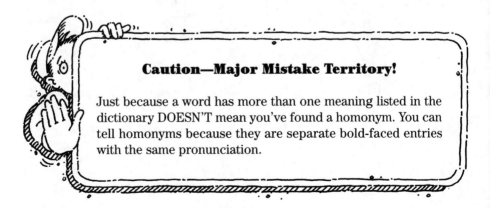

Caution—Major Mistake Territory!

Just because a word has more than one meaning listed in the dictionary DOESN'T mean you've found a homonym. You can tell homonyms because they are separate bold-faced entries with the same pronunciation.

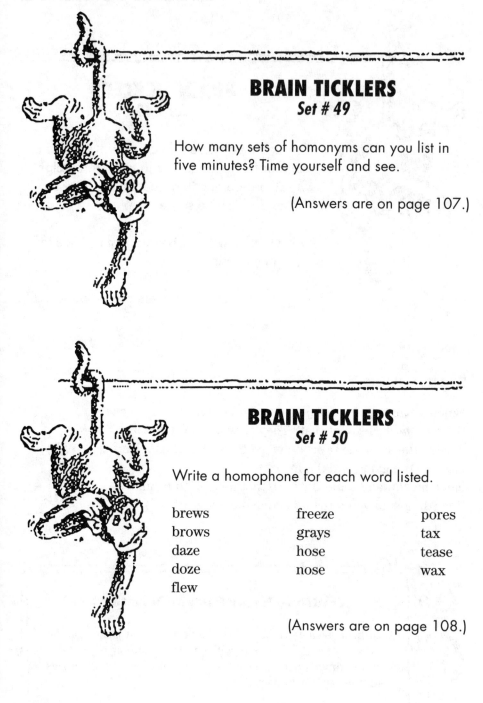

BRAIN TICKLERS
Set # 49

How many sets of homonyms can you list in five minutes? Time yourself and see.

(Answers are on page 107.)

BRAIN TICKLERS
Set # 50

Write a homophone for each word listed.

brews	freeze	pores
brows	grays	tax
daze	hose	tease
doze	nose	wax
flew		

(Answers are on page 108.)

BRAIN TICKLERS— THE ANSWERS

Set # 37, page 84

None of the sets of the words share the same vowel sound.

Set # 38, page 84

1. Possible response (it may vary depending on your dialect):
   sphere, steer, fear
   warm, wore, four
   worm, fir, fur
   dare, welfare, wear

2. Additional word possibilities:
   mere, near, gear
   door, floor, more, core
   brrr, stir, her, incur
   hair, bear, Claire, mare

Set # 39, page 86

/âr/

aer aerosol
air eclair
aire solitaire
ar librarian
are hare

ayer ODDBALL
Can you think of anything besides *prayer?*
ear bear

eir ODDBALL
Can you think of anything besides *heir?*
er sombrero

/îr/

ear sear
eer sneer
eir ODDBALL
Can you think of anything besides *weird?*

eor ODDBALL
Can you think of anything besides *theory?*
er hero
ere revere

ier ODDBALL
Can you think of anything besides *tier?*

/ôr/

ar warn

aur dinosaur

oar boar

oor floor

or forest

ore ignore

our pour

/ûr/

ear ODDBALL
Can you think of anything besides *learn?*

er referee

ere ODDBALL
Can you think of anything besides *were?*

eur connoisseur

ir stirrup

irr ODDBALL
Can you think of anything besides *whirr?*

olo ODDBALL
Can you think of anything besides *colonel?*

or work

our ODDBALL
Can you think of anything besides *courtesy?*

ur burp

urr purr

yrrh ODDBALL
Can you think of anything besides *myrrh?*

Set # 40, page 87

1. avoid, employ, soy
   doubt, Howard, pout
   good, took, would

2. Additional word possibilities:
   coil, annoy, spoil
   cloud, down, proud
   book, could, foot

Set # 41, page 90

Nat and Nate

hug and huge

hid and hide

rag and rage

pin and pine

kin and kine

rat and rate

pop and pope

pan and pane

glad and glade

Set # 42, page 91

Possible responses:
1. lath and lathe
2. wreath and wreathe
3. teeth and teethe
4. bath and bathe

Set # 43, page 92

Possible responses include:

back	rent	mend	dump
pack	sent	fist	rump
tack	tent	gist	bath
camp	bend	list	math
damp	lend	bump	path
lamp			

Set # 44, page 93

silent *b*

bomb	doubt	subtle
catacomb	dumb	succumb
climb	lamb	thumb
comb	limb	tomb
crumb	numb	womb
debt	plumber	

silent *c*
indict

silent *ch*
yacht

silent *d*

grandfather	grandson	sandwich
grandma	handkerchief	veldt
grandmother	handsome	Wednesday
grandpa	landscape	

silent *g*

arraign	diaphragm	impugn
assign	ensign	malign
benign	foreign	paradigm
bologna	gnarled	phlegm
campaign	gnash	poignant
champagne	gnat	reign
cognac	gnaw	resign
cologne	gnome	sign
deign	gnostic	sovereign
design	gnu	

silent *h*

aghast	ghoul	rhododendron
dinghy	myrrh	rhubarb
exhibit	rhapsody	rhyme
ghastly	rhetoric	rhythm
gherkin	rheumatism	sorghum
ghetto	rhinoceros	spaghetti
ghost	rhizome	

silent *k*

knack	knife	knoll
knave	knight	knot
knead	knit	know
knee	knob	knowledge
knell	knock	knuckle
knickers		

silent *l*

could	should	would
palm		

silent *m*

mnemonic

silent *n*

autumn	condemn	hymn
column	government	solemn

silent *p*

cupboard	pseudonym	pterodactyl
pneumatic	psoriasis	ptomaine
pneumonia	psychology	raspberry
psalm	ptarmigan	receipt
psalter		

silent *t*

apostle	glisten	nestle
bristle	gristle	pestle
bustle	hasten	potpourri
castle	hustle	rustle
chasten	jostle	soften
christen	listen	thistle
Christmas	moisten	trestle
epistle	mortgage	wrestle
fasten		

silent *w*

answer	wreck	wrist
sword	wren	write
wraith	wrestle	writhe
wrangle	wretch	wrong
wrap	wriggle	wrote
wrath	wright	wrought
wreak	wring	wrung
wreath	wrinkle	wry

Set # 45, page 94

Possible responses include the following:

1. **bass:** a freshwater fish; a man with a low singing voice; a fibrous plant product

2. **bow:** the front of a ship; to bend one's body in recognition of applause; a rod strung with horsehair and used for playing a string instrument such as a violin

3. **gill:** a fish's respiratory organ; a unit of liquid measure equal to 1/2 cup

4. **lead:** to guide; a soft metal

5. **real:** actually the case; a Portuguese and Brazilian monetary unit

Set # 46, page 95

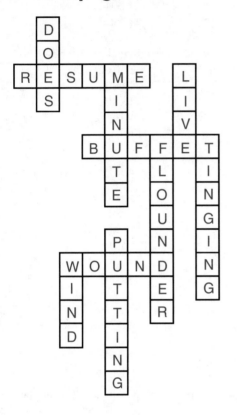

Set # 47, page 98

The Mother Goose rhymes listed are

1. "Little Miss Muffet"

2. "Pussy cat, pussy cat"

3. "Little Bo Peep"

4. "This Little Pig Went to Market"

Set # 48, page 99

Possible responses:

1. Armand Hammer/arm and hammer

2. Hollywood/ha lea would

3. Oh well, I'm ready to race./owe ell lime red eat tour ace

4. Wait until Sam delivers it./weigh ton tills am dee liver zit

Set # 49, page 100

Possible responses:

bank: the earth beside a river; a monetary institution
bark: the sound a dog makes; the covering on a tree trunk
barrow: short for wheelbarrow; a burial mound or hill
bellows: yells loudly; a tool for providing oxygen to a fire
bound: tied up; headed towards
can: a metal container; capable of
champ: to chew; the champion
cricket: a sport; an insect resembling a grasshopper
fare: amount required for a bus/subway/taxi ride; food
fine: a penalty; good
firm: unyielding; a company
fit: a seizure; in good shape, healthy
flat: an apartment; a level
hail: to greet; hard, round precipitation called "hailstones"
hamper: to get in the way of; a container, especially for dirty laundry
last: a shoemaker's tool; the final one
leaves: goes away; the things that fall off trees in autumn
mews: a back street; the noise a cat makes
mine: a deep pit, dug to allow removal of gems and minerals from the earth; something that belongs to me
pants: breathes heavily to reduce internal body temperature; slacks
plane: a two-dimensional surface; a type of tree
quarry: something that's being hunted; a place where stones are mined
rest: a nap; what's left over
rose: a flower; got up
row: an argument; to use an oar or set of oars to propel a boat
stable: steady; a place to keep horses

Set # 50, page 100

brews/bruise
brows/browse
daze/days
doze/doughs
flew/flue
freeze/frieze/frees
grays/graze

hose/hoes
nose/knows/no's
pores/pours
tax/tacks
tease/teas
wax/whacks

Part Two

SYLLABLE JUNCTURES

CHAPTER FIVE

Affixes

SYLLABLE JUNCTURES

Now we're going to shift our focus from vowel and consonant sounds to a more visual approach for a while. We're going to look closely at the points in words where syllables meet, known as *syllable junctures*.

Variety is the spice of syllables

The basic way we characterize syllables is by the pattern of consonant letters and vowel letters that they contain.

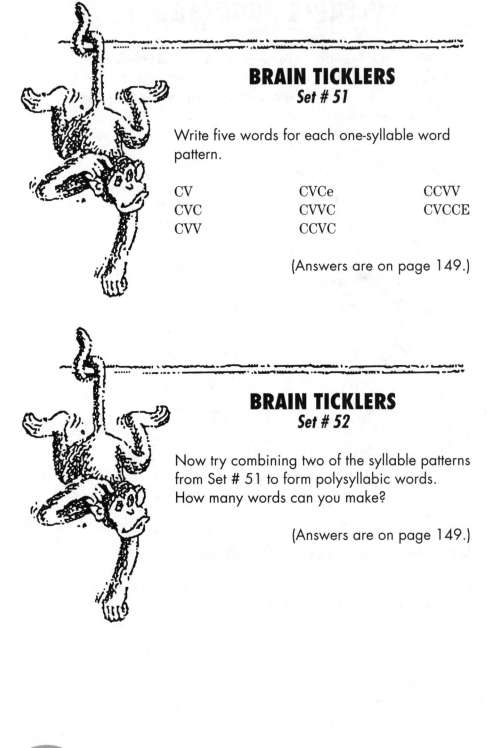

BRAIN TICKLERS
Set # 51

Write five words for each one-syllable word pattern.

CV	CVCe	CCVV
CVC	CVVC	CVCCE
CVV	CCVC	

(Answers are on page 149.)

BRAIN TICKLERS
Set # 52

Now try combining two of the syllable patterns from Set # 51 to form polysyllabic words. How many words can you make?

(Answers are on page 149.)

BRAIN TICKLERS
Set # 53

Since many words have more than one syllable, the patterns get more complex.

1. Write down ten words that have more than
   eight letters.

2. Find their consonant/vowel letter patterns.

3. Say the words aloud. Write down how many syllables each word has.

4. Write about any conclusions you can draw about where syllable junctures occur and about patterns of vowels and consonants.

(Answers are on page 149.)

What good is a syllable juncture?

Syllable junctures (or Sjs) occur within polysyllabic words.
Sometimes it's easier to spell a word if you break it into meaningful parts, and sometimes syllables are meaningful parts that
you might want to use.

Why . . . it wouldn't be the same without Syllable Juncture!

Also, when we add word parts to the beginning or end of words, we create Sjs. And this is where those (probably familiar) rules come in—rules like:

• doubling the consonant

Often a consonant following a short vowel is doubled before adding a suffix to signal the reader that the vowel is to be pronounced in its short form.

hop → hopped, not hoped
/hŏpt/ not /hōpt/

- dropping the final *e*

> Often the silent final *e* that signals a preceding long vowel is dropped before adding a suffix, because the reader will interpret the vowel as long without it, and its presence would affect the pronunciation of the suffix.

hope→ hoped, not hopeed
/hōpt/ not /hŏp ēd/

- changing *y* to *i*

> Often *y* is changed to *i* before a suffix, because otherwise the *y* could be read as a consonant and change the pronunciation of the suffix.

happy→happier, not happyer
/hăp ē ∂r/ not /hăp y∂r/

Knowledge of how syllables fit together will help you become a better speller.

What's in a word?

Let me tell you about some of the vocabulary we'll be using as we explore Sjs.

affix: a word part that cannot stand alone, but must be attached to a base. There are two kinds of affixes: prefixes (like *im-*, *con-*, and *mis-*) and suffixes (like *-ful*, *-arily*, and *-ity*). See below.

base: a word element to which affixes or other bases can be added. It may be a word in itself (*logical*→*illogical*) or not (*cav* meaning "hollow"→ *concave*). Sometimes the word elements that cannot stand alone are called *roots*.

gender: a word's reference to whether its subject is male (like *he*) or female (like *she*). Although they are used less often today, some nouns for occupations traditionally have had both a male and female form (actor, actress; waiter, waitress).

morpheme: the molecule of word study; the smallest unit that has meaning and cannot be subdivided. It can be a base word, like *compute*, a base that is not a word, like *geo*, a prefix like *anti-*, or a suffix like *-s*.

plural: the form of a noun that indicates more than one. Plurals are formed in several ways.

Singular	Plural	Change Made
pig	pigs	+s
mouse	mice	internal change
fish	fish	no change

prefix: an affix that is attached before a base.

root: a source word or word element from which other words or word elements have been formed; what you look for when you hunt down a word's etymology. The word *destroy* comes from the affix *de-* and the root word *struere*, which in English cannot stand alone.

suffix: an affix that is attached to the end of a base. A suffix can change the part of speech of the base (beauty→beautiful), change the tense (sniff→sniffed), change the gender (steward→stewardess), or change the number (pig→pigs).

tense: the indication in a verb of whether it refers to the past, the present, or the future. There are regular and irregular verbs, which change in different ways to create tense.

	Past	Present	Present Perfect
Irregular	sang	sing	has sung
Regular	giggled	giggle	has giggled

BRAIN TICKLERS
Set # 54

Brainstorm as many occupation words that show gender as you can. If there is a form that is not gender-specific, give that also.

(Answers are on page 150.)

Double or nothing

When we change the form of a verb, or adjective, or noun by adding a suffix, this is called *inflection*. We change verbs by adding endings such as *-s, -es, -ed, -en,* and *-ing,* and adjectives by adding endings such as *er* and *est.*

(We'll talk about plurals in the next section.)

BRAIN TICKLERS
Set # 55

Look at each word and its inflected form. Say the words aloud. Form groups that make sense to you. What spelling patterns do you see? What general spelling rules seem to apply to the patterns you found?

big	bigger	rat	ratted
flat	flattest	rate	rating
green	greener	steam	steaming
hop	hopping	stem	stemmed
hope	hoping	traffic	trafficked
hot	hotter	whip	whipping
panic	panicked	wipe	wiped
picnic	picnicking	young	younger
radio	radioed		

(Answers are on page 150.)

PLURALS

Okay, we're going to take our first stab at Sjs (syllable junctures) with forming plurals of English words. This is tricky territory to navigate, because plurals are formed in different ways. Regular plurals are formed by adding -*s* or -*es* to words (rat→rats and veto→vetoes), and irregular plurals may have no change (sheep→sheep) or changes in the middle of the word (goose→geese), or a host of other changes. Your best bet, if you're not sure, is to consult a dictionary.

Do-nothing plurals

This may turn out to be your favorite kind of plural. It's the kind where you look at the singular and … it's identical to the plural so you don't have to do a thing. Here's a list of words in which the singular equals the plural:

aircraft	humankind	samurai
alms	means	scissors
amends	moose	series
bellows	names of tribes and	shambles
chassis	races: Chinese	sheep
deer	offspring	shrimp
fish	pants (slacks)	species
forceps	proceeds	sweepstakes
goods	remains	swine
headquarters	rendezvous	United States

Easy street

This set of plurals follows two easy rules:

1. For most nouns in English, add -s to form the plural.

2. For nouns ending in -ch, -s, -sh, -x, or -z, form the plural by adding -es.

BRAIN TICKLERS
Set # 56

Write the plural for each of the singular nouns listed.

ax	buzz	glass
beach	church	guess
birch	crash	rush
box	dish	waltz
bus	dress	watch
bush	fox	

(Answers are on page 151.)

I say tomatoes, and you say potatoes

Most words that end in Co (consonant, *o*) add -*es* to make the plural.

dingo→dingoes

Words that end in Vo (vowel, *o*) add -*s* to make the plural.

stereo→stereos

Musical terms that come from Italian words and end in Co also add -*s* to make the plural.

alto→altos

Here's a list:
Consonant + *o*
echoes
vetoes
heroes
potatoes
tomatoes
lingoes
Consonant + *o***:** Musical Terms from Italian
cellos
solos
pianos
sopranos
Vowel + *o*
cameos
radios
ratios
rodeos
taboos
ODDBALL
photos

Choose your own plural

Here's another category you might like. For these nouns ending in -*o* you can choose your own plural. Yep, believe it or not, it doesn't matter whether you add -*s* or -*es* to these words. Either way is okay!

I can't decide!

carg**os** or carg**oes**
banj**os** or banj**oes**
grott**os** or grott**oes**
hob**os** or hob**oes**
tornad**os** or tornad**oes**
mosquit**os** or mosquit**oes**
volcan**os** or volcan**oes**
AND this word takes the cake with three acceptable plural
    forms:
buffal**os** or buffal**oes** OR buffal**o**—your choice.

Two different plurals—two different meanings

Some other words have two different plurals, but each plural has a different meaning. Here's a list for you to look at.

Singular	Plural # 1 and Meaning	Plural # 2 and Meaning
brother	brothers (two boys born to the same parents)	brethren (members of the same society, e.g., the Quakers)
die	dies (tools used to stamp)	dice (numbered cubes used for games)
genius	geniuses (brilliant people)	genii (imaginary spirits, like the one in Aladdin)
index	indexes (tables of contents)	indices (algebraic signs)
staff	staves (poles or supports; the five-line systems on which music is written)	staffs (groups of assistants)

What's the difference between a dwarf and an elf?

The difference is that you form the plural of *dwarf* by adding *-s* (*dwarfs*) and the plural of *elf* by changing *f* to *v* and adding *-es* (*elves*). Here's the rule:

+ s   −f + v + es

All words ending in *f(e)* (that means either final *f* like *dwarf* or *fe* like *café*) add *s* to make the plural with the following exceptions, which change *f* → *v* and add *-es* (or if they end in *e* already, just add *-s*):

calf	calves	self	selves
elf	elves	sheaf	sheaves
half	halves	shelf	shelves
knife	knives	thief	thieves
leaf	leaves	wife	wives
life	lives	wolf	wolves
loaf	loaves		

The three ODDBALLS in this group are *wharf, scarf,* and *hoof.* For these three words, you can add either *-s* or change *f* to *v* and add *-es*, whichever you like. And, just for the record, words ending in a double *ff* (except *staff*, which has two plurals—see page 130—and *dandruff*, which isn't clearly singular or plural and has no plural form) all take the *-s* ending. For example:

sheriffs
tariffs
mastiffs

How wise are you . . .

. . . when it comes to making plural forms for nouns ending in -*y*? Here are the rules:

If the noun ends in Vy (vowel, *y*) add -*s*.

decoy→decoys

If the noun ends in Cy (consonant, *y*) or a consonant sound and *y* (for example, in *colloquy*, in which the *qu* sounds like /kw/), change -*y* to -*i* and add -*es*.

bunny→bunnies

BRAIN TICKLERS
Set # 57

Write the plural for each noun listed below.

beauty	donkey	soliloquy
bunny	french fry	Sunday
buy	guy	tray
city	monkey	turkey

(Answers are on page 151.)

Why can't the Romans learn to pluralize?

Foreign words can have unusual plurals, because although there may be a "regular" plural formed with -s or -es, the preferred plural is from their original language. This chart will give you an idea of some of the Latin words involved.

Singular	Plural
alumnus	alumni (us → i)
cactus	cacti
fungus	fungi
nucleus	nuclei
radius	radii
analysis	analyses (is→ es)
basis	bases
crisis	crises
diagnosis	diagnoses
hypothesis	hypotheses
bacterium	bacteria (um→ a)
datum	data
medium	media
ovum	ova
alumna	alumnae (a→ae)
antenna (insect feelers)	antennae
larva	larvae
vertebra	vertebrae
matrix	matrices (ix→ices)
criterion	criteria (on→a)

BRAIN TICKLERS
Set # 58

Use the patterns in the previous chart to form the plurals of the following words:

antithesis	oasis	referendum
dictum	optimum	serum
focus	parenthesis	streptococcus
gladiolus	phenomenon	ulna
memorandum		

(Answers are on page 151.)

Major renovations: inside out plurals

These are the words that change in the middle, rather than at the end.

Singular	Plural
child	children
foot	feet
goose	geese
tooth	teeth
louse	lice
mouse	mice
man	men
woman	women
ox	oxen
person	people

Which word takes the s?: plurals of compound words

Simple—usually you just pick the main noun and form its plural as you would if it stood alone. So:

attorney-at-law→attorneys-at-law

bachelor's degree→bachelor's degrees

man-of-war→men-of-war

mother-in-law→mothers-in-law

passer-by→passers-by

runner-up→runners-up

step-child→step-children

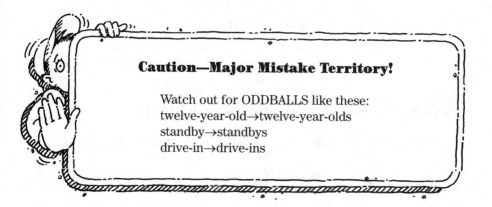

Caution—Major Mistake Territory!

Watch out for ODDBALLS like these:

twelve-year-old→twelve-year-olds

standby→standbys

drive-in→drive-ins

Plurals of proper names: Podhaizers, Yendrzeskis, Nguyens, and Dinwiddies

Hi!
Have you seen the
Dinwiddies?

What's a
Dinwiddies?

This is so simple that some people think it's complicated. Here's the rule:

> If the proper noun ends in *ch*, *s*, *sh*, *x*, or *z* in the singular, add *-es*. Otherwise, just add *-s*, even if the word ends in Cy (consonant, *y*).

Singular	Plural
Adonis	Adonises
Denny	Dennys
Szymkowicz	Szymkowiczes
Choothamkhajorn	Choothamkhajorns
Mansfield-Marcoux	Mansfield-Marcouxes

Plurals of letters, dates, numbers, signs, and abbreviations

Easy . . . for the first four groups, just stick on apostrophe and -*s*, like this:

Singular	Plural
x	x's
1990 (the year)	1990's
&	&'s
3	3's

For an abbreviation with periods, add an apostrophe and -*s*. If it has no periods, just add -*s*:

YMCA→YMCAs
Ph.D.→Ph.D.'s
Co.→Co.'s

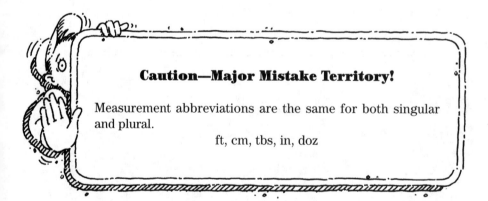

Caution—Major Mistake Territory!

Measurement abbreviations are the same for both singular and plural.

ft, cm, tbs, in, doz

SIMPLE PREFIXES

Philosopher Gregory Bateson once stated as one of the fundamental principles of education: "The Division of the Perceived
Universe into Parts and Whole is Convenient and May Be Necessary, . . . But No Necessity Determines How It Shall Be Done."
Sometimes textbooks do a disservice by slicing things only one
way. Looking at the same object of study from multiple perspec-
tives may give you a greater understanding. We're going to call
this:

Slicing and dicing

We can talk about prefixes in a number of different schemas.

If we talk about their:	we can gain insight into:
etymological source	the words they would likely be combined with
part of speech	the kind of word they will be attached to
meaning	how to use them

So we could talk about Greek prefixes (etymology); prefixes that
are prepositional, adjectival, and adverbial (part of speech); or
the prefixes *micro-* and *mini-*, which both mean small (meaning). Or we could just list them all alphabetically.

BRAIN TICKLERS
Set # 59

Study this list of 47 prefixes (we'll deal with the other type, called "assimilated prefixes," later). Group them in a way that makes sense to you, such as using one of the chart categories on the left of the previous chart. You may find a dictionary helpful for this. Write a sentence or two about how you organized prefixes.

a-	without, not
a-	on, in
a-	up, out, away
amphi-	around, both
anti-	against, opposite

Caution—Major Mistake Territory!

When anti- precedes a base word starting with a vowel letter, you usually add a hyphen, as in *anti-American*. But for the word *antacid*, you drop the *i*. Another oddball is *cata-* in the word *category*—it loses its final *a*.

auto-	self
be-	around, about, away, thoroughly
bi-	two, twice

cata-	down, away, against
circum-	around, on all sides
contra-	against
counter-	opposite
de-	reversal, removal, away, from, off, down
dia-	through, together
equi-	equal
eu-	good, pleasant
extra-	beyond, outside
hemi-	half
hyper-	extra, over, excessive, beyond
hypo-	under, beneath, below
inter-	among, between
intra-	within
macro-	large
mal-	bad, wrongful
micro-	very small
mis-	wrongly, badly, not correct
multi-	many
neo-	new
non-	against, not, without
out-	to a greater degree, located externally or outside
over-	over, excessively
para-	beside, similar to, beyond
peri-	about, around
post-	after, following
pre-	before
pro-	forward, in place of, favoring
pseudo-	false, pretended, not real
re-	again, back, backward
retro-	back, backward
semi-	half, twice
super-	above, extra, over
trans-	across, beyond
tri-	three, every third
ultra-	beyond, excessively
un-	not, opposing
under-	below, beneath
uni-	one

(Answers are on page 152.)

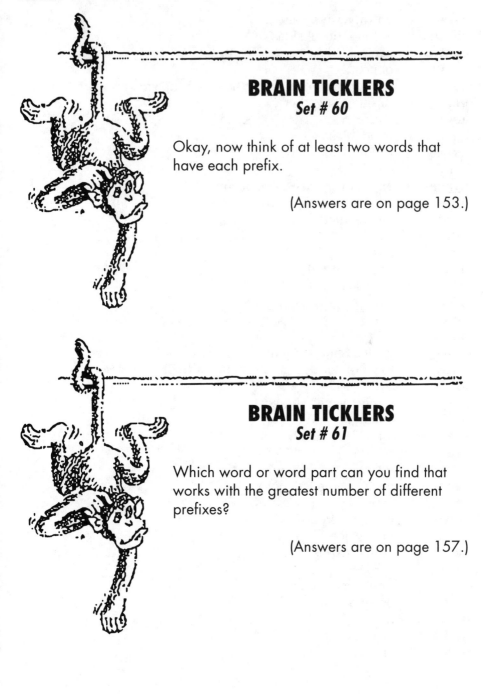

BRAIN TICKLERS
Set # 60

Okay, now think of at least two words that have each prefix.

(Answers are on page 153.)

BRAIN TICKLERS
Set # 61

Which word or word part can you find that works with the greatest number of different prefixes?

(Answers are on page 157.)

BRAIN TICKLERS
Set # 62

Using the words you've collected in Set # 60 and Set # 61, make up a list of the spelling rules that would help you. Give example words to demonstrate each rule.

(Answers are on page 157.)

SIMPLE SUFFIXES

America's most wanted

What suffix do you think is most used? I haven't found any statistics about this, but if -*ed* isn't the most frequently used suffix, it's certainly up there. Let's take a look at -*ed* and its sound.

MOST

– ed   suffix

WANTED

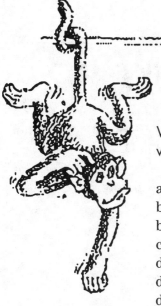

BRAIN TICKLERS
Set # 63

Write the past tense for each verb listed. What visual patterns do you notice?

arrest	flap	lie
bat	fight	pot
boil	grade	press
catch	graze	rat
dare	greet	sail
deal	hop	sleep
dial	kneel	slop
divide	lace	snag
fix	lent	track

(Answers are on page 157.)

BRAIN TICKLERS
Set # 64

For each word in Set # 63, write another word with the same visual pattern that forms the past tense in the same way. Then if you can, write another word that has a similar visual pattern but forms its past tense in a different way. Write a sentence or two about your findings.

(Answers are on page 158.)

141

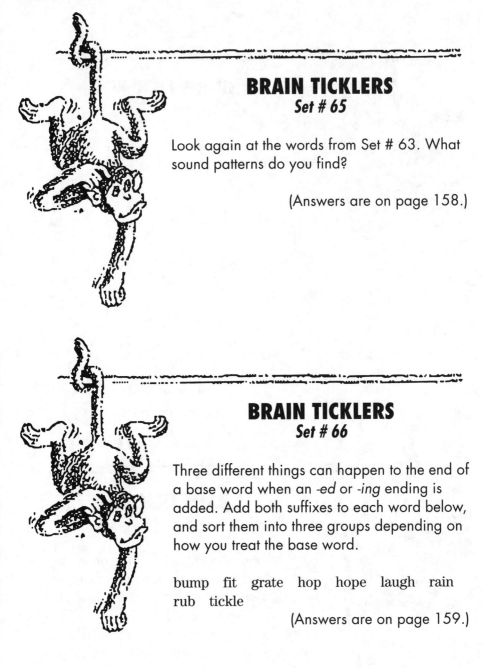

BRAIN TICKLERS
Set # 65

Look again at the words from Set # 63. What sound patterns do you find?

(Answers are on page 158.)

BRAIN TICKLERS
Set # 66

Three different things can happen to the end of a base word when an *-ed* or *-ing* ending is added. Add both suffixes to each word below, and sort them into three groups depending on how you treat the base word.

bump   fit   grate   hop   hope   laugh   rain   rub   tickle

(Answers are on page 159.)

Suffix survey

Slicing, dicing, mincing, chopping, and blending

We could talk about suffixes in even more different schemas
than we had for prefixes.

Whoah!

If we talk about their:	we can gain insight into:
etymological source	the base words they would likely be combined with
forms	how to attach them to the base word or word part they go with
meaning	how to use them
function	the effect they have on the base word they are attached to (e.g., turning a verb into a noun)

So we could talk about Latin suffixes (etymology); the suffix /ə/ and its various spellings (forms); suffixes that mean where a person is from, like -*er* and -*ian* (meaning); or the suffix -*tion* that can turn the verb *civilize* into the noun *civilization* (function). Or we could just list them all alphabetically.

Let's start with the **function** of making an adverb. Besides past tense suffixes and plurals, the adverbial suffix -*ly* is probably one of the most common suffixes. Some things adverbs with -*ly* endings can do are tell how (helplessly), to what extent (frequently), how much (slightly), and when (weekly).

This is how you add the endings to adjectives or nouns to make adverbs:

Word Ending	Change to Make Adverb	Sample
consonant *y*	change *y* to *i* and add -*ly*	clumsy→clumsily
consonant *e*	drop *e* and add -*ly*	gentle→gently
double *l*	drop one *l* and add -*ly*	dull→dully

Suf-fixation

Now let's talk about the **function** of making a noun. How many suffixes do you think there are that indicate nouns? There are at least 90! Ninety is too many to discuss at once, so let's narrow it down to some subcategories.

BRAIN TICKLERS
Set # 67

1. For each name of a PLACE listed below, add a suffix to form the noun that names a person who comes from that place. Use this model:

   A person who comes from America is an _____, but be careful, because not all of these nouns are formed with the same suffix.

(Use a dictionary if necessary.) Make a list of the different suffixes you used.

Nigeria   Iraq   Hungary   Panama   Vermont   Japan

2. When you add a suffix to most nouns, there are four possibilities:
   - no change: hold + ing→ holding
   - double the final consonant and add the suffix: hop + ing→ hopping
   - drop the final e and add the suffix: hope + ing→ hoping
   - change y to i and add the suffix

But with place names, there can be different kinds of changes. Look at these groups of nouns that indicate a place with which a person is associated. What was done to the name of each place before the suffix was added?

Swedish   Finnish   Polish   Turkish   English   Irish   Spanish

Canadian   Peruvian   Chilean   Mexican   Italian   Jordanian

Chinese   Balinese   Javanese   Vietnamese   Taiwanese

Bengali   Israeli   Kuwaiti   Saudi

(Answers are on page 159.)

145

BRAIN TICKLERS
Set # 68

Here are some suffixes that are part of words that tell what PEOPLE do, activities they are involved in, their vocations, or their hobbies. For each suffix, write at least one word that has that suffix. What changes did you make as you added the suffixes?

-aire	-eer	-ian
-ant	-ent	-ist
-ee	-er	-or

(Answers are on page 159.)

BRAIN TICKLERS
Set # 69

The noun suffixes listed below have to do with ideas, characteristics, attitudes, beliefs, and feelings—all ABSTRACT concepts. Read the definition and the sample word for each suffix.

1. What changes occurred in the base words as the suffixes were added?

2. Put the red words into the puzzle.

-ation state, condition, or quality of	isolate→isolation
-cy a quality or condition	dependence→dependency
-dom the condition of being ___	free→freedom
-hood state, condition, or quality of being	brother→brotherhood
-ics the science or art of	ethos→ethics
-ism a doctrine or system or principle	Buddha→Buddhism
-ment action or state	judge→judgment
-ness state, quality, or condition of being	kind→kindness
-red the condition of	hate→hatred
-ship quality or condition of	friend→friendship
-tude a condition or state of being	gratis→gratitude
-ty, ity a condition or quality	animus→animosity

(Answers are on page 160.)

BRAIN TICKLERS— THE ANSWERS

Set # 51, page 114

CV: my, he, no, go, we
CVC: pig, hog, pen, cob, mud
CCV: sty, she, cry, two, gnu
CVV: May, hue, lie, boo, key
CVCe: hope, pure, love, give, vale
CVCC: sign, mold, park, warm, Turk
CCVC: know, stem, Kris, shut, Fred
CVVC: jail, boat, been, pour, boil
CCVV: free, blue, thou, flea, whoa
CVCCE: purse, horse, tense, range, bathe

Set # 52, page 114

Answers will vary. Possible responses:

CV CV	mama
CVC CVC	market
CVC CVV	coffee
CV CVVC	reboot
CVV CVV	mayday
CVV CVC	Dayton
CVC CV	manly
and so on	

Set # 53, page 115

Possible responses:
1, 2, and 3:
unanimous: VCVCVCVVC; 4 syllables
imagination: VCVCVCVCVVC; 5 syllables
understanding: VCCVCCCVCCVCC; 4 syllables
calliopes: CVCCVVCVC; 4 syllables
innovation: VCCVCVCVVC; 4 syllables
independent: VCCVCVCCVCC; 4 syllables
cauliflower: CVVCVCCVCVC; 4 syllables
melancholy: CVCVCCCVCV; 4 syllables
farsighted: CVCCVCCCVC; 3 syllables
optimistic: VCCVCVCCVC; 4 syllables

4. Observations: Vowels tend to appear singly (34 times), but occasionally can be found in groups of two (4 times), whereas consonants come in groups of two (12 times) and groups of three (3 times) and also appear singly (27 times).

Often the sound of the word splits between the double or within the triple syllable. Syllables with short vowels seem to often both begin and end with consonants. Syllables with long vowels seem to end with the vowel.

Set # 54, page 120

Possible responses:

Male Form	Female Form	Non-Specific Form
businessman	businesswoman	business person
chairman	chairwoman	chair
cowboy	cowgirl	cowhand
farmer	farmerette	farmer
fireman		fire fighter
garbage man		sanitation worker
mailman; postman		mail carrier; postal worker
shepherd	shepherdess	shepherd
steward	stewardess	flight attendant
usher	usherette	usher

Set # 55, page 121

1. If you are adding -ed or -ing to a word ending in -ic, double the consonant by adding a k.

panic	panicked
picnic	picnicking
traffic	trafficked

2. If you are adding an ending to a word with a short vowel followed by a single consonant, double that consonant.

hop	hopping	big	bigger
rat	ratted	flat	flattest
stem	stemmed	hot	hotter
whip	whipping		

3. If you are adding an ending to a word with a short vowel already followed by two consonants, simply add the ending.

young younger

4. If you are adding an ending to a word with a long vowel, simply add the ending, or if the word ends in silent -e, drop the e and add the ending.

hope	hoping	steam	steaming
radio	radioed	wipe	wiped
rate	rating	green	greener

Set #56, page 123

axes	buzzes	glasses
beaches	churches	guesses
birches	crashes	rushes
boxes	dishes	waltzes
buses	dresses	watches
bushes	foxes	

Set # 57, page 129

beauties	donkeys	soliloquies
bunnies	french fries	Sundays
buys	guys	trays
cities	monkeys	turkeys

Set #58, page 131

antitheses	oases	referenda
dicta	optima	sera
foci	parentheses	streptococci
gladioli	phenomena	ulnae
memoranda		

Set # 59, page 136

Possible response: I grouped the prefixes by language of origin:

Old English

a- on, in
a- up, out, away
be- around, about, away, thoroughly
mis- wrongly, badly, not correct

out- to a greater degree, located externally or outside
over- over, excessively
un- not, opposing

Greek

a- without, not
amphi- around, both
anti- against, opposite
auto- self
bi- two, twice
cata- down, away, against
dia- through, together
eu- good, pleasant
hemi- half

hyper- extra, over, excessive, beyond
hypo- under, beneath, below
macro- large
micro- very small
neo- new
para- beside, similar to, beyond
peri- about, around
pseudo- false, pretended, not real

Latin

circum- around, on all sides
contra- against
counter- opposite
de- reversal, removal, away, from, off, down
equi- equal
extra- beyond, outside
inter- among, between
intra- within
mal- bad, wrongful
multi- many
non- against, not, without
post- after, following

pre- before
pro- forward, in place of, favoring
re- again, back, backward
retro- back, backward
semi- half, twice
super- above, extra, over
trans- across, beyond
tri- three, every third
ultra- beyond, excessively
under- below, beneath
uni- one

Set # 60, page 138

Possible responses:

Old English

Prefix	Meaning	Examples
a-	on, in	abed, aboard, afoot, asleep
a-	up, out, away	arise, awake
be-	around, about, away, thoroughly	behead, beloved, beset
mis-	wrongly, badly, not correct	misapply, misinterpret, mismanage, misspell, mistake
out-	to a greater degree, located externally or outside	outboard, outdo, outhouse, outlive, outshine, outshoot
over-	over, excessively	overcompensate, overdrive, overdue, overrun, oversee
un-	not, opposing	unaccompanied, undo, unhappy, unlock, untrue

Greek

Prefix	Meaning	Examples
a-	without, not	amoral, apolitical
amphi-	around, both	amphibious amphitheater
anti-	against, opposite	antibody, antiseptic, antipathy
auto-	self	autobiography, automobile
bi-	two, twice	bicycle, bimonthly
cata-	down, away, against	cataclysm, catastrophe
dia-	through, together	dialogue, diameter
eu-	good, pleasant	eulogy, euphemism
hemi-	half	hemiplegic, hemisphere
hyper-	extra, over, excessive, beyond	hypercritical, hypertension, hyperthermia
hypo-	under, beneath, below	hypocritical, hypodermic, hypothesis
macro-	large	macrobiotic, macrocosm
micro-	very small	microcosm, micromanage, microscope
neo-	new	neolithic, neologism, neonatal, neo-Nazi
para-	beside, similar to, beyond	paragraph, paranormal, paraphrase, paraprofessional
peri-	about, around	perimeter, periscope
pseudo-	false, pretended, not real	pseudonym, pseudopod, pseudoscience

Latin

Prefix	Meaning	Examples
circum-	around, on all sides	circumference, circumnavigate
contra-	against	contradict, contraindicated
counter-	opposite	counteract, counterrevolution
de-	reversal, removal, away, from, off, down	deactivate, decapitate, decode, decrease, delouse, demean, destroy
equi-	equal	equidistant, equilateral, equivalent
extra-	beyond, outside	extracurricular, extraordinary, extraterrestrial
inter-	among, between	intermurals, international, interplanetary, interstate
intra-	within	intramurals, intramuscular, intravenous
mal-	bad, wrongful	malalignment, malignant, malodorous, maltreatment
multi-	many	multicolored, multiform, multimillionaire, multinational
non-	against, not, without	nonentity, nonessential, nonexistent, nonsense, nonstop, nonviolence
post-	after, following	postdate, postgraduate, postpone, postscript

Prefix	Meaning	Examples
pre-	before	preclude, prefix, preheat, prejudge
pro-	forward, in place of, favoring	proclaim, prolong, pronoun, prorevolution
re-	again, back, backward	reappear, relinquish, repair, repay, replace
retro-	back, backward	retroactive, retrorocket, retrospect
semi-	half, twice	semiannual, semicircular, semidetached, semiformal
super-	above, extra, over	supernatural, supersaturated, superscript, superstar
trans-	across, beyond	transcontinental, transpolar, transport
tri-	three, every third	triangle, tricycle, trimonthly
ultra-	beyond, excessively	ultraconservative, ultramodern, ultrasonic, ultraviolet
under-	below, beneath	underground, underhanded, underwater, underwear
uni-	one	unicycle, unison

Set # 61, page 138

Possible responses:
do: outdo, overdo, undo
cycle: bicycle, tricycle, recycle, unicycle
critical: diacritical, hypercritical, uncritical
logue: catalogue, dialogue, prologue
monthly: bimonthly, trimonthly, semimonthly
vert: controvert, extrovert (or extravert), revert
verse: converse, reverse, transverse, universe
scribe: circumscribe, describe, proscribe, transcribe
script: postscript, prescript, superscript, transcript,
spect: circumspect, prospect, respect, retrospect

Set # 62, page 139

Possible response:

1. When adding a prefix to a base that begins with the same letter the prefix ends with, you will have a double letter: *misspell, overrun, counter-revolution*

2. When adding a prefix that ends in a vowel letter to a base that begins with a vowel letter, you will have a double vowel letter: *contraindicated, deactivate, extraordinary, reappear, retroactive, semiannual, triangle*

3. When adding a prefix to a base that begins with a capital letter, use a hyphen and keep the capital letter capitalized: *anti-American, neo-Nazi*

4. In almost every case, the prefix is spelled exactly the same way, no matter what base it is added to: *deactivate, decapitate, decode, decrease, delouse, demand, destroy,* and so on.

Set #63, page 141

End in *ed*

arrested	flapped	potted
batted	graded	pressed
boiled	grazed	ratted
dared	greeted	sailed
dialed	hopped	slopped
divided	laced	snagged
fixed	lied	tracked

End in -t

caught	fought	lent
dealt	knelt	slept

Set # 64, page 141

End in -ed

arrested	nested	flapped	trapped	potted	dotted
batted	ratted	graded	faded	pressed	dressed
boiled	toiled	grazed	hazed	ratted	batted
dared	scared	greeted	heated	sailed	mailed
dialed	mailed	hopped	stopped	slopped	cropped
divided	bided	laced	faced	snagged	dragged
fixed	nixed	lied	died	tracked	backed

End in _t_

caught	taught	watched
dealt		healed/stole
fought		lighted/lit
knelt	felt	peeled
lent	bent/sent	tended
slept	crept/kept	peeped/seeped

Set # 65, page 142

Past tenses ending in -ed with the sound /t/:

fixed	laced	slopped
flapped	pressed	tracked
hopped		

Past tenses ending in -ed with the sounds /id/:

graded	greeted	ratted
potted	batted	divided
arrested		

Past tenses that end in -ed and have the sound /d/:

boiled	grazed	sailed
dared	lied	snagged
dialed		

Past tenses ending in -t that end with the sound /t/:

bent	fought	lent
caught	kept	slept
dealt	knelt	

Set # 66, page 142

no change	double final consonant	drop final *e*
bumped, bumping	fitted, fitting	grated, grating
laughed, laughing	hopped, hopping	hoped, hoping
rained, raining	rubbed, rubbing	tickled, tickling

Set # 67, page 145

1. Nigerian Iraqi Panamanian Vermonter Japanese
      -n   *-i*   *-nian*   *-er*   *-ese*

2. Sweden→ Swedish   Finland→Finnish   Poland→Polish
   Turkey→Turkish   England→English   Ireland→Irish
   Spain→Spanish

   Canada→Canadian   Peru→Peruvian   Chile→Chilean
   Mexico→Mexican   Italy→Italian   Jordan→Jordanian

   China→Chinese   Bali→Balinese   Java→Javanese
   Vietnam→Vietnamese   Taiwan→Taiwanese

   Bengal→Bengali   Kuwait→Kuwaiti   Saudi→Saudi
   Israel→Israeli

None of these groups can be explained by a single rule. The first two are very complicated groups.

Set #68, page 146

commisionaire legionnaire millionaire (These words come from French, and in French they all have a double *n* as in *legionnaire*. In French, it's *millionnaire* and *commissionnaire*. *Billionaire* is an exception—it doesn't come from French. It is an English word formed on the model of *millionaire*, so it doesn't have a double *n* form. The English word *questionnaire* also retains the double *n* from French.)

debutant	assistant	descendant
referee	employee	appointee
engineer	auctioneer	rocketeer
student	correspondent	superintendent
farmer	reporter	dancer
physician	musician	phonetician
typist	novelist	pianist
actor	aviator	investigator

Set # 69, page 147

drop the *e*: isolate; dependence; judge; hate
no change: free; brother; kind; friend
drop the *-os*: ethos
drop the *-a*: Buddhism
drop the *-s*: gratis
drop the *-us*: animus

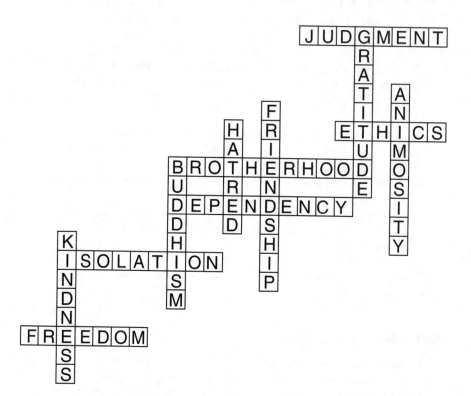

CHAPTER SIX

COMPOUND INTEREST

Compound words are words made up of two or more whole words, not just word parts or elements. In this way, compound words are different from words with one or more affixes attached. *Antidisestablishmentarianism* is a long, sophisticated word, but it's not a compound word. It's a word with two prefixes, a base word, and four suffixes:

Prefixes	**Base**	**Suffixes**
Anti- dis-	establish	-ment -arian (-ary + -an) -ism

Bye-bye is a short, childish word, but it's still a compound word.

BRAIN TICKLERS
Set # 70

1. Group the following compound words in categories that make sense to you.

2. Write a sentence or two explaining your categories.

best seller
bridegroom
bull's-eye
cross-country skiing
emerald green
great-great-uncle
how-to book
ice cream

one-half mile
problem solving
stick-in-the-mud
toothache
vice-president
whiteout
whole-wheat bread

(Answers are on page 170.)

Biography of a compound

We generally distinguish three categories of compound words: **open** (in which there is space between the words); **hyphenated** (in which they are connected by a hyphen); and **closed** (in which the words are run together). In general, compounds begin their life together just sitting next to each other in sentences. This casual association happens so often, that people recognize it and make the relationship of the words more formal by putting a hyphen between them. As the relationship continues, the words are thought of in such close connection that they become joined forever.

It is my personal opinion that some compound words stay in the hyphen stage and never become closed simply because they would be too difficult to read closed up.

Jack-in-the-pulpit (a woodland plant) is a lot easier to read at a glance than Jackinthepulpit. Even its shorter name, Indian turnip, looks pretty funny stuck together: Indianturnip.

To hyphenate or not to hyphenate: that is the question

Some words that exist as compounds with a particular meaning can also exist on their own with a very different meaning. In these cases, how you connect the words can give your sentence two VERY different interpretations. My favorite example is from *Words Into Type*, page 227. Compare these two sentences:

> She used a camel's-hair brush.
> She used a camel's hairbrush.

Which would you rather use on your hair?

Sometimes capital letters can help distinguish a compound word.

> He lives in the white house.

is way different from

> He lives in the White House.

BRAIN TICKLERS
Set # 71

Draw a picture for each sentence.

1. Wow! What a hot house!

2. Wow! What a hothouse!

3. That man is my great-grandfather.

4. That man is my great grandfather.

5. The house full of people began to dance.

6. The houseful of people began to dance.

7. She is an ancient Chinese scholar.

8. She is an Ancient Chinese scholar.

(Answers are on page 170.)

You can count on it

Because compound words go through a progression, becoming more closely linked the longer they stay together, the best way to know how to spell a compound is to look in a current dictionary. Some rules for compounds, however, are always true. And some of these rules are about using hyphens with numbers.

1. Spell all compound numbers from twenty-one to ninety-nine with hyphens.
   twenty-one
   ninety-nine

2. Spell all fractions used as adjectives with hyphens.
   two-thirds of a foot
   three-tenths of a mile

3. Spell all compound adjectives that contain a cardinal number followed by a noun or adjective with hyphens.
   nine-foot board
   one-sided argument
   two-hundred-dollar keyboard

4. Spell all compound adjectives that contain an ordinal number followed by a noun with a hyphen.
   third-story room
   first-class accommodations

BRAIN TICKLERS
Set # 72

Form as many compounds as possible by combining words from the following list:

break	full	shine
day	light	stop
fast	moon	sun

(Answers are on page 171.)

BRAIN TICKLERS—
THE ANSWERS

Set # 70, page 164

1. Possible response:
   - best seller   emerald green   ice cream   problem solving
   - bridegroom   toothache   whiteout
   - bull's-eye   cross-country   skiing   great-great-uncle   how-to book
     vice-president   one-half mile   stick-in-the-mud
   - whole-wheat bread

2. Possible response: Some of the compounds are run together, some have a space between them, some are connected by a hyphen, and one has a hyphen between two of its words and space between the other two.

Set # 71, page 167

Answers in art:

1.

2.

3.

4.

5.

6.

7.

8.

Set # 72, page 169

full moon
moonshine
sunshine
full stop
stoplight
sunlight
daylight
daybreak
breakfast
fast day

Part Three

DERIVATIONAL CONSISTENCY

Derivation tells us where something comes from.
It's the same idea as etymology.
When we trace the derivation of a word,
we learn about the language in which it originated
and how it came into English. In this section we
will work toward understanding how a word's
appearance can give us clues that help us
understand meaning or sound.

CHAPTER SEVEN

Alternations

CHANGES IN SOUND

Pastry shop: what's under the crust?

Whether you prefer pie, calzone, ravioli, doughnuts, or pierogi, if you've ever bought a closed pastry you may have experienced that moment of doubt—it looks like all the others, but what's really inside? All the pastries look the same, but are they the same? There are some words like those pastries—words that look alike, but aren't pronounced alike. Fortunately, these words follow some rules of pronunciation, so they are identifiable.

Here's an example. Look at these words:

sign	signature	signer
signal	signed	signing
signatory		

All the words have the letters **s-i-g-n** in them. They look like they should be pronounced in a similar way, but if you try saying them, you'll see that they're not. The letters stay the same to help you understand that the words have related meanings. But watch out when you spell them! Sometimes you hear the /g/ sound, and sometimes you don't, but you always have to write it. Do you remember the term *inert letter* (from Chapter 4)? **Inert letters** are letters that appear in a word segment every time it occurs, sometimes heard, and sometimes not. The *g*'s that you don't hear but have to write are inert letters.

This may seem complicated or frustrating because you have to write letters that you don't hear when you say the word. But that *g* is actually useful. Here's why. Say there wasn't a *g* in the word *sign*. Then you'd spell it *s-i-n*, right? Now the complications are even greater. Is the word *sin*, /sin/ meaning "an offense against God" or *sin*, /sin/ the abbreviation in trigonometry for *sine*, or /sin/ the twenty-first letter of the Hebrew alphabet, or is it *si[g]n* /sin/?

The word **morpheme** names a unit of language, like *sign*, that has a stable meaning and cannot be divided into smaller parts. It is kind of like a molecule—the smallest possible example of a compound.

The word *pig* is a single morpheme.

Piglet has two morphemes: *pig* and the diminutive suffix *-let*.

Pigheaded has three: *pig* and *head* and *-ed*, a suffix which makes it an adjective.

Pigheadedness has four, including *-ness*, a suffix meaning "a state or quality of being."

English tries to keep a single spelling for a single morpheme, even when the pronunciation changes.

BRAIN TICKLERS
Set # 73

For each set of words in the following list, identify the letter that is silent in one or some words and sounded in the other(s).

resign	resignation	
malign	malignant	
condemn	condemnation	
soft	soften	softly
economical	economically /ĕc ∂ nŏm ĭ k lē/	

Reminder: The ∂ represents the schwa sound—the unaccented sound that is voiced like short *u*.

debt	debit	
doubt	dubious	
grand	grandma /gr ăm mä/	
hand	handsome	handkerchief

(Answers are on page 186.)

Everybody SH!

There are other situations in which words sound different but are obviously connected in meaning and spelling. One case is when suffixes pronounced / ∂n/ are added to words that end in *ic* or *t*. Once you add that ending, the *c* or *t* no longer sounds as itself, but assumes a /sh/ sound. For example, we say *connect* with a /t/ at the end, but in *connection*, we hear /sh/ and no /t/.

In British English, they change the spelling to show this: *connexion*.

The easy part for spelling is that these words just add *-ion* or *-ian* at the end, keeping their same last letter,
as in *connect→connection* or *physic→physician*.
Or, if they end in *-te*, they drop the *e* and add *-ion*.
as in *delete→deletion*.

BRAIN TICKLERS
Set # 74

Add an *-ion* or *-ian* ending to each word below. Underline the letter that is seen but not heard.

academic	considerate	invent
adopt	contort	logistic
assert	demonstrate	magic
associate	discriminate	music
attract	electric	pediatric
circulate	except	reflect
clinic	inhibit	select
complete	inspect	
composite	instruct	

We'll talk more about *-ion* and *-ian* endings later.

(Answers are on page 186.)

Shorting out

In "Everybody SH!" you saw that sometimes spelling doesn't reflect the pronunciation changes that occur at the final syllable juncture when you add a suffix to a word. In the cases we looked at there, there was a change in the pronunciation of the final consonant sound in the base. In some words, there is a change in the pronunciation of a vowel in a particular syllable, although the spelling in that syllable stays the same. In one group of words, a schwa pronunciation changes to a short vowel pronunciation with the addition of a suffix. Remember that schwa has the sound of short *u* in an unaccented syllable. Let's look at how the schwa-to-short vowel change works.

Take the words *local* and *legal*. They are each accented on the first syllable, which is pronounced with a long vowel:

LO cal   LE gal

The vowel in the second syllable is a schwa. Listen to what happens when you add the ending -*ity*. The accented syllable changes to the second syllable.

lo CAL i ty   le GAL i ty

Because schwa exists only in UNaccented syllables, the sound of the second syllable CAN'T be schwa anymore, so the sound returns to the short vowel /ă/. But the spelling doesn't change.

BRAIN TICKLERS
Set # 75

Notice how you can add the suffix indicated to each base word. Underline the accented syllable in the resulting word. Identify the vowel sound you hear in that syllable.

central + ity = centrality
economy + ics = economics
formal + ity = formality

metal + ic = metallic
relative + ity = relativity

(Answers are on page 186.)

Shorting out two

Under certain circumstances, adding a suffix can change the pronunciation of a long vowel to a short vowel—again, without a spelling change.

Take the word *please*. It has a long vowel in the accented syllable:

PLEASE

Listen to what happens when you add the ending *-ant*. The accented syllable stays the same, but the long vowel becomes short:

PLEAS ant

BRAIN TICKLERS
Set # 76

Notice how you can add the suffix indicated to each base word. Underline the accented syllable in the resulting word. Identify the vowel sound you hear in that syllable.

bile + ious = bilious
cone + ic = conic
crime + inal = criminal
diabetes + ic = diabetic

divine + ity = divinity
mime + ic = mimic
sane + ity = sanity
serene + ity = serenity

state + ic = static
tone + ic = tonic
volcano + ic = volcanic

(Answers are on page 187.)

All things being equal

Do you remember that the word *schwa* comes from a Syriac word meaning "equal"—maybe because many different sounds are kind of "equalized" into one sound (more or less) in unstressed syllables? When you add a suffix to a base word, and the accentuation of the word changes so that a syllable that was stressed is no longer stressed, a vowel with a long pronunciation can end up being pronounced as a schwa. The spelling stays the same so that you can recognize that the words are related, but the sound changes.

Take the word *compete*. It has a long vowel in the second syllable, which is accented:

com PETE

Listen to what happens when you add the ending -*ition*. The accented syllable changes, and the long vowel sound becomes a schwa:

com pe TI tion

BRAIN TICKLERS
Set # 77

Notice how you can add the suffix indicated to each base word. Underline the accented syllable in the resulting word. Identify the change in vowel sound that occurred. What do all the base words have in common? Add two of your own, if you can.

admire + ation = admiration
coincide + ent = coincident
define + ition = definition

preside + ent = president
reside + ent = resident

(Answers are on page 187.)

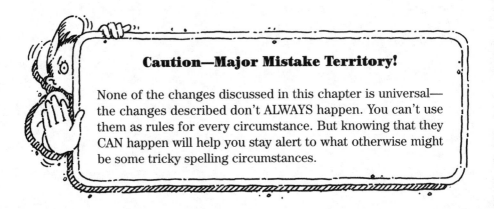

Caution—Major Mistake Territory!

None of the changes discussed in this chapter is universal—the changes described don't ALWAYS happen. You can't use them as rules for every circumstance. But knowing that they CAN happen will help you stay alert to what otherwise might be some tricky spelling circumstances.

BRAIN TICKLERS—
THE ANSWERS

Set # 73, page 179

g	resign	resignation	
g	malign	malignant	
n	condemn	condemnation	
t	soft	soften	softly
a	economical	economically	
b	debt	debit	
b	doubt	dubious	
d	grand	grandma	
d	hand	handsome	handkerchief

Set # 74, page 181

academician
adoption
assertion
association
attraction
circulation
clinician
completion
composition

consideration
contortion
demonstration
discrimination
electrician
exception
inhibition
inspection
instruction

invention
logistician
magician
musician
pediatrician
reflection
selection

Set # 75, page 183

centrality	short a
economics	short o
formality	short a
metallic	short a
relativity	short i

Set # 76, page 184

bi<u>li</u>ous	short *i*
<u>co</u>nic	short *o*
<u>cri</u>minal	short *i*
dia<u>be</u>tic	short *e*
di<u>vi</u>nity	short *i*
<u>mimi</u>c	short *i*
<u>sani</u>ty	short *a*
se<u>re</u>nity	short *e*
<u>stati</u>c	short *a*
<u>toni</u>c	short *o*
vol<u>cani</u>c	short *a*

Set # 77, page 185

admi<u>ra</u>tion	long *i* goes to *∂*
co<u>in</u>cident	long *i* goes to *∂*
defi<u>ni</u>tion	long *i* goes to *∂*
<u>pres</u>ident	long *i* goes to *∂*
<u>res</u>ident	long *i* goes to *∂*

Possible responses: perspire→ perspiration inspire →inspiration

CHAPTER EIGHT

Homophonous Endings

SAME SOUND, DIFFERENT LOOK

Did you ever notice that many suffixes with identical sounds are spelled different ways? In this chapter we will sort out some of these homophonic suffixes so that you can understand them better.

Pay attenssion! I mean, pay attencian! Oh, just pay attention!

There are two ways of trying to sort out the /ən/ endings in order to make sense of them: one is by sight, and the other is by sound. We will try both. You should know to begin with that the following suffixes are in this group:

-sion   -ssion   -tion   -cion   -ician   -en

BRAIN TICKLERS
Set # 78

Look at the base word and the resulting word with the /∂n/ ending.

1. Write the word made by adding the identified suffix.

2. Give the group of words a name based on how they end.

3. Tell what conclusion you can draw about how words in this grouping take an /∂´n/ ending.
   A. All these groups take the -*sion* ending:
      a. decide   invade
      b. confuse   repulse
      c. express   regress   succeed
   B. All these words take the -*tion* ending:
      a. admire   imagine   inspire
      b. suppose   compose   expose
      c. combust   exhaust   suggest
      d. inspect   instruct   reflect
   C. All these words take the -*ian* ending:
      a. magic   mathematic   music   politic   statistic

(Answers are on page 207.)

Sound it out

Another approach to /ǝn/ words focuses on sound and meaning.
-*ician* and -*en* are meaning groups as well as visual groups:

-*ician* refers to a person and his/her profession, specialty, or
practice.
A *magician* is someone who is skilled in magic.
A *dietician* is a person who is professionally qualified to give
guidance about diet.

-*en* creates a verb concerned with a meaning related to causing
or becoming from an adjective:
cheap→cheapen   quick→quicken
OR, it forms a verb showing cause or possession from a noun:
length→lengthen

This leaves us with -*sion, -ssion, -tion,* and -*cion* to distinguish.

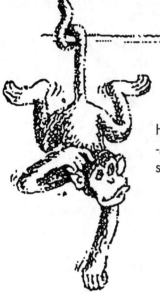

BRAIN TICKLERS
Set # 79

Here is the list of words from Set # 78 with the *-ician* words eliminated. Try sorting them by sound: /chən/, /shən/, or /zhən/.

admire	admiration	inspire	inspiration
combust	combustion	instruct	instruction
compose	composition	invade	invasion
confuse	confusion	reflect	reflection
decide	decision	regress	regression
exhaust	exhaustion	repulse	repulsion
expose	exposition	succeed	succession
express	expression	suggest	suggestion
imagine	imagination	suppose	supposition
inspect	inspection		

(Answers are on page 207.)

We are us, ous, ious, eous

Delicious, scrumptious, and *nutritious*! How *generous* of you to share this treat with me without *animus.* Sounds delectable, right? But how do you know when to use which spelling of /∂s/? We'll try to sort out this knotty-naughty homophonic problem.

And without animus, too!

- *-ous, ious,* and *-eous* all mean "characterized by or full of."
- *-us* is a singular Latin ending (the plural end is *-i*). It appears in words like:

alumnus	alumni
cactus	cacti
fungus	fungi
nucleus	nuclei
radius	radii

so its meaning puts it in a separate category from the other endings.

- Let's focus on *-ous, -iou,s* and *-eous* for a bit. When you attach them to a word, you can immediately hear the difference. Words like:
  generous, callous, preposterous, and *joyous*, all with an /∂s/ sound, sound different than
  fallacious /sh∂s/, *flirtatious* /sh∂s/, and *courteous* /ē∂s/
- So we're left trying to tell when to use *-cious* and when to use *-tious*. *-cious* is a lot more common, so that should help, for starters. Besides that, look at the base word and see if you can make connections.

BRAIN TICKLERS
Set # 80

For each group of words, write an observation about adding *-ious* or *-eous* to it.

-atious

flirtation   flirtatious

vexation   vexatious

-acious

capacity   capacious

audacity   audacious

sagacity   sagacious

mendacity   mendacious

-nious

harmony   harmonious

ceremony   ceremonious

felony   felonious

-eous

spontaneity   spontaneous

nauseate   nauseous

-itious

nutrition   nutritious

ambition   ambitious

-icious

malice   malicious

avarice   avaricious

caprice   capricious

office   officious

suspicion   suspicious

(Answers are on page 208.)

Are you responsIBLE for choosing a suitABLE ending?

-able and *-ible* are a complicated pair.

May I introduce able and ible.

Look at the following rules:

1. Most times that the ending is added to a whole word, you use *-able*, and when it is added to a base that cannot stand alone as a word, you add *-ible*.

Whole Word		Non-Word	
depend	dependable	aud	audible
break	breakable	ed	edible

2. If the base word ends in silent *e*
   a. preceded by a soft *c* /s/ or *g* /j/, keep the *e* and add *-able*.
      manage   manageable
      notice   noticeable
   b. without a soft *c* or *g*, drop the *e* and add *-able*.
      love   lovable
      use   usable

3. If the *-ion* form of the word is
   a. spelled *-ation*, add *-able.*

admire	admiration	admirable
tolerate	toleration	tolerable
transport	tranportation	transportable

   b. spelled without an *a*, add *-ible*, even though it IS a whole word.

contract	contraction	contractible
produce	production	producible

   c. spelled with *ss* or *ns*, add *-ible* after the *ss* or *ns*.

permit	permission	permissible
transmit	transmission	transmissable

There are some exceptions and additions to these rules (like *collapse,* which ends in silent *e,* but becomes *collapsible*), but these guidelines should stand you in pretty good stead.

BRAIN TICKLERS
Set # 81

Write the *-able* or *-ible* form of the following words:

admit	commend	read
apply	comprehend	vis-
blame	contract	
change	leg- /lej/	

(Answers are on page 209.)

Getting a hand/ǝl/ on /ǝl/

/ǝl/ can be spelled *el*, *le*, *al*, and occasionally *il* and *ol* (endings in *-ful* aren't included here). Some of them are recognizable as being *-acle*, *-icle*, or *-ical*.

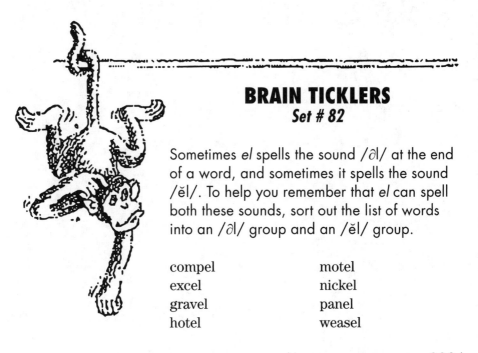

BRAIN TICKLERS
Set # 82

Sometimes *el* spells the sound /ǝl/ at the end of a word, and sometimes it spells the sound /ĕl/. To help you remember that *el* can spell both these sounds, sort out the list of words into an /ǝl/ group and an /ĕl/ group.

compel	motel
excel	nickel
gravel	panel
hotel	weasel

(Answers are on page 209.)

Grueling rules

All spellings occur for a reason. But the /əl/ words have so many reasons for their different spellings that there's no simple way to categorize them. Practicing with the words is the best way to see how they work. So let's practice.

BRAIN TICKLERS
Set # 83

Find as many /əl/ words as you can in the word find on page 201. (There are 59.) Group them by the spelling of the /əl/ sound: el, le, al, il, ol, -acle, -icle, or -ical.

```
E L M P E N C I L L O E L A L O L I L A C L E E L
L E A E L C O C L I L V U L A L V E T L A C L E I
E L P E L A L I A E L W A F F L E E U O D D R A L
L E L E O M M C E R O L I L A C H E N R I U M M E
P R E T Z E L L E L O N K E M L I P N M M R R S S
L R E L U L D E D N D L L E M A C L E P P A R R F
H H E L Q R A S A N D A L A C L L E L E L E G G E
I S M M U P T T G G D L A T C L E E L E E R O C L
S E L C L E E L K E N N L I N I T I A L E A C C Z
T P P O N O L L E L D N A C N L O L L E D D U O O
O R I C M M A L R P L E L K E L E E L G N I J L O
R R I N B M B B N P P L L L E L B A F F C C U O B
I L E L A L M M E I L E L E F F B L F L E A M N M
C E L M O L Y I L R H M A C K E R E L E L L B E A
A V L L A C C A E S M A M M A L L T T L A O L L B
L I A O L R N L U S E L E G O B B L E L R R E S S
D N V B B G B B E L L A L A P B A S I L T L O Q E
D S I P E M M L S S K G G L A U B S E N N O D U L
F F T L U E Y L E I N N P L L B B V L E E D D I C
F E S B L E E S L G I E L U E L O L E L C I T R A
F E E L E S S U M N W A L O D H U L C L E L E R T
S E F L L E L T T A T L N E E D L E L E L E L E N
E S C O U N D R E L L I L O L E L A L I C L E L E
C E L A L I L O L U L A C L E I C E L C A R I M T
```

(Answers are on page 210.)

And the rooster said, "ər, ər, ər, ər, ər!"

The first thing you need to know is that some words that we spell with an *-er* suffix are spelled in British English with an *-re* suffix, and these spellings are often listed in the dictionary. Here are some examples:

American Spelling	British Spelling
theater	theatre
center	centre
fiber	fibre
liter	litre
meter	metre
somber	sombre
caliber	calibre
saber	sabre

The American /ər/ words differ in the sound that precedes /ər/ and in having two different spellings: -er and -ure.

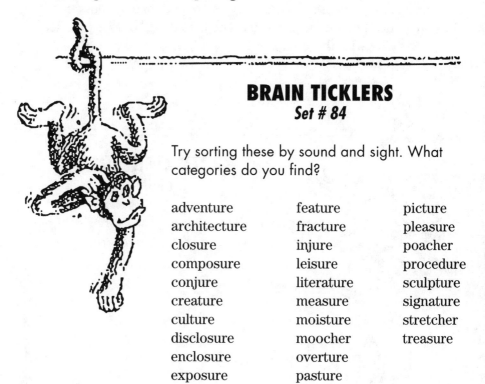

BRAIN TICKLERS
Set # 84

Try sorting these by sound and sight. What categories do you find?

adventure	feature	picture
architecture	fracture	pleasure
closure	injure	poacher
composure	leisure	procedure
conjure	literature	sculpture
creature	measure	signature
culture	moisture	stretcher
disclosure	moocher	treasure
enclosure	overture	
exposure	pasture	

(Answers are on page 211.)

Don't let this be an instANCE for your impatiENCE

Some words take the ending -ent, and others take -ant. Some take -ence, whereas others take -ance. Some take -ency, and others take -ancy. Fortunately, words like *compete* that take -ent, also take -ence AND -ency.

compete   competent   competence   competency

And words like *hesitate* that take -ant, also take -ance AND -ancy.

hesitate   hesitant   hesitance   hesitancy

So once you know if a root word takes an *a* or an *e* in these endings, you're set. BUT . . . not every word can take all three suffixes. And sometimes the suffixes are attached to roots that cannot stand alone as words. The best thing to do is practice working with the groups.

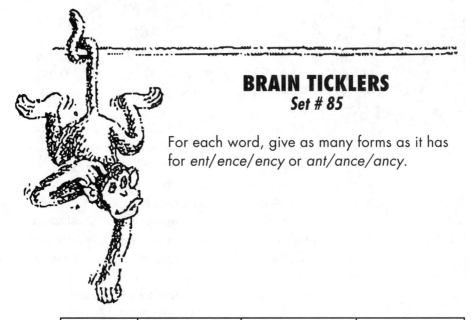

BRAIN TICKLERS
Set # 85

For each word, give as many forms as it has for *ent/ence/ency* or *ant/ance/ancy*.

Starter	ant/ent form	ance/ence form	ancy/ency form
accept			
allow			
annoy			
buoy			
coincide			
confide			
converse			

Starter	ant/ent form	ance/ence form	ancy/ency form
correspond			
depend			
differ			✕
dominate			
emerge			
equal			
excel			
exist			✕
expect			
grief	✕		✕
hesitate			
ignore			✕
import			✕
infant	✕	✕	
magnify			✕
obey			
persist			
recur			✕
rely			✕
revere			✕
signify			✕
vibrate			
violate			✕

(Answers are on page 212.)

BRAIN TICKLERS
Set # 86

Some *ent/ence* words are pretty rare. For extra credit . . . over and above the call of duty, look up these five *ent/ence* words and note their meanings. Use the biggest dictionary you can find. (They're all in the *Oxford English Dictionary.*)

attingence   comburence   frugiferent
lutulence   regredience

(Answers are on page 212.)

BRAIN TICKLERS—
THE ANSWERS

Set # 78, page 192

Words ending in *-de*, drop the *-de* and add *-sion*.
invade   invasion
decide   decision

Words ending in *-se*, drop the *se* and add *-sion*.
confuse   confusion
repulse   repulsion

Words ending in *-ss*, drop an *s* and add *-sion*.
express   expression
regress   regression
success   succession

Words ending in silent *e* not specified above, drop the *e* and add an *a* before *-tion*.

admire	admiration
imagine	imagination
inspire	inspiration

Words ending in *-se*, drop the *e* and add an *-i* before *-tion*.

suppose	supposition
compose	composition
expose	exposition

Words ending in *-ct* or *-st*, drop the *-t* and add *-tion*.

combust	combustion
exhaust	exhaustion
inspect	inspection
instruct	instruction
reflect	reflection
suggest	suggestion

Words that end in *-ic* name professions. Add *-ian*.

magic	magician
mathematic	mathematician
music	musician
politic	politician
statistic	statistician

> These visual groups can help you predict spelling, but there are exceptions. For example, *intend*, *contend*, and *attend* (and some others) take *-tion*, rather than *-sion*. *Compose* and *expose* (and some others) take *-ition* rather than *-ation*.

Set # 79, page 194

/chən/

combust	combustion
exhaust	exhaustion
inspect	inspection
instruct	instruction
reflect	reflection
suggest	suggestion

/sh∂n/

admire	admiration
compose	composition
expose	exposition
express	expression
imagine	imagination
inspire	inspiration
regress	regression
succeed	succession
suppose	supposition

/zh∂n/

confuse	confusion
decide	decision
invade	invasion
repulse	repulsion

Set # 80, page 196

Answers may vary. Possible responses:

-atious
Words that have an -*ation* form take -*atious*.

flirtation	flirtatious
vexation	vexatious

-acious
Words that have a -*acity* form take -*acious*.

capacity	capacious
audacity	audacious
sagacity	sagacious
mendacity	mendacious

-nious
Words that have an -*ony* form take -*nious*.

harmony	harmonious
ceremony	ceremonious
felony	felonious

-eous
Words with an *e* after the last consonant in the root take *i*.

spontaneity	spontaneous
nauseate	nauseous

-itious
Words with an *-ition* form take *-itious*.
nutrition   nutritious
ambition   ambitious

-icious
Words with an *-ic(e)* take *-icious*.
malice   malicious
avarice   avaricious
caprice   capricious
office   officious
suspicion   suspicious

Set # 81, page 198

admit   admissible
apply   applicable
blame   blamable
change   changeable
commend   commendable
comprehend   comprehensible
contract   contractible
leg- /lej/   legible
read   readable
vis-   visible

Set # 82, page 199

/ĕl/
compel   hotel
excel   motel

/əl/
gravel   panel
nickel   weasel

Set # 83, page 200

```
E  L  M  P  E  N  C  I  L  L  O  E  L  A  L  O  L  I  L  A  C  L  E  E  L
L  E  A  E  L  C  O  C  L  I  L  V  U  L  A  L  V  E  T  L  A  C  L  E  I
E  L  P  E  L  A  L  I  A  E  L  W  A  F  F  L  E  E  U  O  D  D  R  A  L
L  E  L  E  O  M  M  C  E  R  O  L  I  L  A  C  H  E  N  R  I  U  M  M  E
P  R  E  T  Z  E  L  L  E  L  O  N  K  E  M  L  I  P  N  M  M  R  R  S  S
L  R  E  L  U  L  D  E  D  N  D  L  L  E  M  A  C  L  E  P  P  A  R  R  F
H  H  E  L  Q  R  A  S  A  N  D  A  L  A  C  L  L  E  L  E  L  E  G  G  E
I  S  M  M  U  P  T  T  G  G  D  L  A  T  C  L  E  E  L  E  E  R  O  C  L
S  E  L  C  L  E  E  L  K  E  N  N  L  I  N  I  T  I  A  L  E  A  C  C  Z
T  P  P  O  N  O  L  L  E  L  D  N  A  C  N  L  O  L  L  E  D  D  U  O  O
O  R  I  C  M  M  A  L  R  P  L  E  L  K  E  L  E  E  L  G  N  I  J  L  O
R  R  I  N  B  M  B  B  N  P  P  L  L  L  E  L  B  A  F  F  C  C  U  O  B
I  L  E  L  A  L  M  M  E  I  L  E  L  E  F  F  B  L  F  L  E  A  M  N  M
C  E  L  M  O  L  Y  I  L  R  H  M  A  C  K  E  R  E  L  E  L  L  B  E  A
A  V  L  L  A  C  C  A  E  S  M  A  M  M  A  L  L  T  T  L  A  O  L  L  B
L  I  A  O  L  R  N  L  U  S  E  L  E  G  O  B  B  L  E  L  R  R  E  S  S
D  N  V  B  B  G  B  B  E  L  L  A  L  A  P  B  A  S  I  L  T  L  O  Q  E
D  S  I  P  E  M  M  L  S  S  K  G  G  L  A  U  B  S  E  N  N  O  D  U  L
F  F  T  L  U  E  Y  L  E  I  N  N  P  L  L  B  B  V  L  E  E  D  D  I  C
F  E  S  B  L  E  E  S  L  G  I  E  L  U  E  L  O  L  E  L  C  I  T  R  A
F  E  E  L  E  S  S  U  M  N  W  A  L  O  D  H  U  L  C  L  E  L  E  R  T
S  E  F  L  L  E  L  T  T  A  T  L  N  E  E  D  L  E  L  E  L  E  L  E  N
E  S  C  O  U  N  D  R  E  L  L  I  L  O  L  E  L  A  L  I  C  L  E  L  E
C  E  L  A  L  I  L  O  L  U  L  A  C  L  E  I  C  E  L  C  A  R  I  M  T
```

LE

bamboozle	fable	puddle
bubble	gobble	ripple
bumble	jingle	rumple
camel	jumble	tattle
candle	maple	tickle
curdle	marble	turtle
dimple	needle	twinkle
eagle	pretzel	waffle

ACLE

miracle   tentacle

ICLE

article   icicle   vehicle

ICAL

historical   radical

AL

central   mammal   signal
cymbal   opal   spinal
festival   oval
initial   sandal

EL

angel   hovel   scoundrel
bushel   kernel   snivel
camel   mackerel   squirrel
colonel   mussel   tunnel

OL

carol   idol   symbol

IL

basil   pencil   stencil

Set # 84, page 203

Two Syllables
/ch∂r/
creature   moisture   poacher
culture   moocher   sculpture
feature   pasture   stretcher
fracture   picture

/zh∂r/
closure   measure   treasure
leisure   pleasure

/j∂r/
conjure   injure

Three or More Syllables
/ch∂r/
adventure   literature   signature
architecture   overture

/zh∂r/

composure	enclosure	exposure
disclosure		

/j∂r/

procedure

Set # 85, page 204

accept	acceptant	acceptance	
allow		allowance	
annoy		annoyance	
buoy	buoyant	buoyance	buoyancy
coincide	coincident	coincidence	
confide	confident	confidence	
converse	conversant	conversance	conversancy
correspond	correspondent	correspondence	correspondency
depend	dependent	dependence	dependency
differ	different	difference	
dominate	dominant	dominance	dominancy
emerge	emergent	emergence	emergency
equal	equivalent	equivalence	equivalency
excel	excellent	excellence	excellency
exist	existent	existence	
expect	expectant	expectance	expectancy
grief		grievance	
hesitate	hesitant	hesitance	hesitancy
ignore	ignorant	ignorance	
import	important	importance	
infant			infancy
magnify	magnificent	magnificence	
obey	obedient	obedience	
persist	persistent	persistence	persistency
recur	recurrent	recurrence	
rely	reliant	reliance	
revere	reverent	reverence	
signify	significant	significance	
vibrate	vibrant	vibrance	vibrancy
violate	violent	violence	

Set # 86, page 206

attingence: influence
comburence: ability to cause combustion, that is, start a fire
frugiferent: bearing fruit
lutulence: muddiness
regredience: return

CHAPTER NINE

Greek and Latin Base Words

FAMILY RESEMBLANCE

In Chapter 5 we talked about prefixes with Greek and Latin origins, as well as Latin plurals. But since many important base words come to us from Greek and Latin and form the basis of some hefty word families, we're going to take some time to focus on them. The important point from a spelling perspective is that these word families all have a family resemblance, kind of like everyone in a family having curly hair or freckles—some feature that helps you identify that they go together. For the

most part, once you know the spelling of a base, there is not a lot of variation. If you can spell *metr/meter*, the Greek root meaning "measure," you can spell it in *symmetry, diameter, metric, geometry, thermometer,* and so on. Familiarity with these widely used roots will improve your spelling.

BRAIN TICKLERS
Set # 87

Just to get you started . . . take a look at these root words and their meanings. Write as many English words that have each root word as you can. You can use a dictionary if you wish. Remember that you can have the root word appear at the beginning, middle, or end of an English word, and you can add prefixes, suffixes, or both to it.

Greek	Meaning	Example
aster/astr	star	astronaut
auto	self	automatic
chron	time	chronic
graph	writing	paragraph
Latin		
scrib/script	to write	scribe
voc/vok	to call/voice	vocal chords
verb	word	verbal
son	sound	sonic

(Answers are on page 228.)

Sound familiar?

It's easier to remember a group of interconnected words than just a random list of roots. So let's look at some logically connected groups of root words. First let's focus on words having to do with sound.

Sound

Root Word	Meaning	Language of Origin	Example
phe/phem	speak	Greek	euphemism
dic/dict	speak	Latin	dictate
lingu	language/tongue	Latin	linguistic
gloss/glott/glot	tongue/language	Greek	polyglot
phon	sound	Greek	phonograph
aud	hear	Latin	audible
ora	speech/mouth	Latin	oracle

BRAIN TICKLER
Set # 88

How many words can you discover that have at least one of the above root words in it?

(Answers are on page 229.)

Vision revision

Many English words having to do with looking, seeing, the eye, and tools used with the eye have Greek and Latin roots.

Sight

Root Word	Meaning	Language of Origin	Example
photo/phos	light	Greek	photograph
luc	light	Latin	lucid
scope	instrument for viewing	Greek	microscope
spect	look	Latin	prospect
vid/vis	to see	Latin	video
ops/opt/op	sight; eye	Greek	optical
ocul	eye	Latin	ocular

BRAIN TICKLERS
Set # 89

This time, tell the meaning of each word made from one of the "sight" roots.

photograph	phosphorescent
telescope	elucidate
inspect	monocle
invisible	ophthalmologist

Look up the word in a dictionary if you need to.

(Answers are on page 229.)

The law of the land

Just as our legal system and our system of government have their origins in Greece and Rome, so do many words having to do with right and justice (the judicial branch) and governing (the executive branch) come from these two civilizations.

Hey! Watch your step!

Right/Justice

Root Word	Meaning	Language of Origin	Example
jud	judge	Latin	judge
val	strong/worth	Latin	valuable
ortho	correct/straight	Greek	orthopedics
crit/cris	judge	Greek	critical
dox	opinion	Greek	paradox
eth	moral	Greek	ethos
nom	law	Greek	Deuteronomy
soph	wise	Greek	sophisticated
bon/ben	good	Latin	bonus
mal	bad	Latin	malfunction

Governing

Root Word	Meaning	Language of Origin	Example
pol/polis	city, state	Greek	politics
arch	rule/govern	Greek	matriarch
cracy	rule/government	Greek	autocracy
ethn	nation	Greek	ethnicity
dem	people	Greek	epidemic

BRAIN TICKLERS
Set # 90

Read each clue and write the word containing one of the "Law of the Land" roots that fits into the crossword puzzle. Notice which spelling is used for the roots that have alternate forms.

Down

1. Accepting an established doctrine

4. To evaluate

5. The absence of a ruler

6. Wrongdoing by someone who holds public office

7. Not legally valid

8. Having to do with a major city

Across

2. Principles of moral value

3. Having to do with courts of law

9. Working for the good of

10. Reasoning that appears wise, but isn't

11. Rule by the people

12. Relating to racial and cultural heritage

13. Rule of a single person by him/herself

(Answers are on page 230.)

To life!

Life

Root Word	Meaning	Language of Origin	Example
spir	to breathe	Latin	perspire
zoo	animal	Greek	zoo
dendr/dender	tree	Greek	dendrology
anim	spirit/life	Latin	animated
vit/viv	life	Latin	vital

While at the zoo, the dendrologist
began to perspire when the vital life
form became a little too animated.

BRAIN TICKLERS
Set # 91

Put the words from the list below into the puzzle to make the mystery word appear in the vertical box.

animal
inspiration
rhododendron

spirit
vivid
zoology

Mystery word clue:

It originally meant "those who share a stream" and now means "competitors." Name this word that comes from a Latin root.

(Answers are on page 230.)

Miscellaneous but not extraneous

Here are three more categories—size, love, and study—and a challenge to go with them.

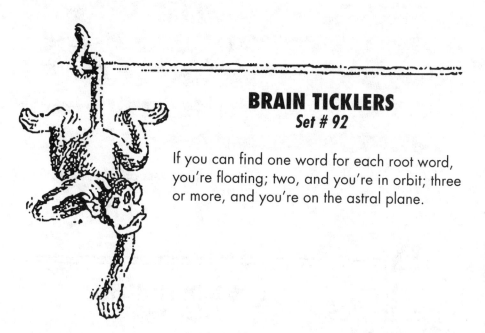

BRAIN TICKLERS
Set # 92

If you can find one word for each root word, you're floating; two, and you're in orbit; three or more, and you're on the astral plane.

Size

Root Word	Meaning	Language of Origin
micro	small	Greek
mega/megalo	large	Greek
magna	large	Latin

Love

Root Word	Meaning	Language of Origin
philo	love	Greek
ama/ami	love	Latin

Study

Root Word	Meaning	Language of Origin
logo	word/reason	Greek
doc/doct	teach	Latin
sci	know	Latin
gno/gnos	know	Greek
ver	truth	Latin

(Answers are on page 231.)

BRAIN TICKLERS
Set # 93

Now it's time to review what you've learned. Write a composition in which you use at least ten words, each having a different Greek or Latin root used in this chapter. You can write a short story, a news story, a diary entry, or any other kind of piece that strikes your fancy. But choose your topic carefully to make your work easier.

(Answers are on page 231.)

BRAIN TICKLERS
Set # 94

The final challenge . . . Can you take some of the prefixes from Chapter 5 and combine them with the roots here to make new words? Use clues to help you. Combine Greek prefixes with Greek roots and Latin prefixes with Latin roots. Use a dictionary to help you if you need to.

Greek Prefixes	Clues Make words that mean:
a- (an-) without, not	"not knowing" "without leadership"
anti- against, opposite	"against the law; opposition"
auto- self	"rule by a single person"
dia- through, together	"to talk together"
eu- good, pleasant	"a pleasant way of speaking about an unpleasant topic"
hyper- extra, over, excessive, beyond	"overcritical"
micro- very small	"an instrument that enlarges a small sound"
para- beside, similar to, beyond	"beyond opinion"
peri- about, around	"an instrument that allows one to look around corners"
pseudo- false, pretended, not real	"with a false appearance of refinement"

Latin Prefixes	Clues
bi- two	"having two lenses, for both eyes"
circum- around, on all sides	"to look around; prudent"
de- reversal, removal, away, from, off, down	"to reduce the value of"
multi- many	"able to speak many languages"
pre- before	"to evaluate before sufficient evidence is available"
re- again, back, backward	"to look at again in order to correct" "to make move again" "to make live again"
trans- across, beyond	"something which light shines through" "to breathe out"

(Answers are on page 232.)

BRAIN TICKLERS— THE ANSWERS

Set # 87, page 216

Possible responses:

Greek	
aster/astr	astronomy asteroid astronomer asterisk astral astrocyte astrodome astrodynamics astrogate astrology astrometry astronautics astronavigation astrophotography astronomical astrophysics astrosphere
auto	automobile autobiography autograph autobiographer autochrome autochton autoclave autocrat autoharp autohypnosis automat autonomy autopsy

chron	chronicle synchrony chronology chronometer chronograph
graph	autograph biography autobiography photograph telegraph bibliography graphic grapheme calligraphy

Latin

scrib/script	script describe inscribe transcribe transcript manuscript prescription
voc/vok	vocal evoke advocate vociferous revoke provoke equivocate vocabulary vocalist vocation invocation
verb	verbal verbalize verbatim adverb proverb
son	sonnet sonorous dissonance resonance

Set # 88, page 218

phe/phem blaspheme
phon telephone, phonics, symphony, euphony, polyphony, cacaphony, aphonic, orthophonic, megaphone, microphone
dic/dict diction, dictator, dictionary, contradict, contradiction, indict, benediction, edict, malediction
aud auditory, auditorium, inaudible, audience, audio, audition
lingu linguine(!), bilingual, lingo, linguist
ora oral, oration, oratorio
gloss/glott/glot glossolalia, gloss, glossary

Set # 89, page 219

photograph: a print made on light-sensitive paper
telescope: an instrument to see things that are far away
inspect: to look at closely
invisible: not able to be seen
phosphorescent: permitting emission of light after exposure to radiation
elucidate: to bring to light; to make plain
monocle: a single lens used to improve vision
ophthalmologist: a physician specializing in the function and diseases of the eye

Set # 90, page 221

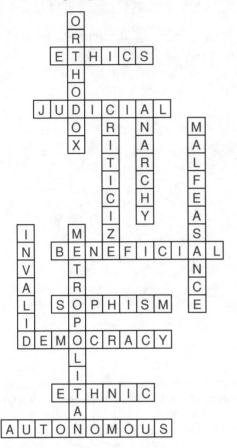

Set # 91, page 224

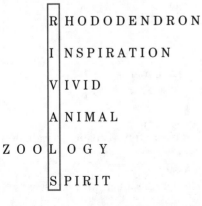

The words spell *rivals*, which is the mystery word.

Set # 92, page 225

Size

micro	microphone micromanage microeconomics microbiology microelectronics microbe microchip
mega/megalo	megaphone megabucks megahertz megabyte megavitamin
magna	magnanimous magnify magnitude magnate magnificent

Love

philo	philodendron philosophy philology philanthropy philately hemophilia
ama/ami	amateur amicable amity amiable amigo

Study

logo	logic analogy catalogue dialogue monologue prologue eulogy archaeology genealogy geology syllogism analogy
doc/doct	doctrine documentary doctor docudrama docile indoctrinate
sci	science omniscient prescience scientist scientific
gno/gnos	agnostic prognosticate gnosticism
ver	veracity verify verisimilitude veracious verity verdict

Set # 93, page 226

Possible response: a poem

Once there was an <u>astronaut</u>, who also was a <u>polyglot</u>.

He went on many <u>astral</u> trips in spaceships that used <u>microchips.</u>

He wasn't one to cry or mope. He <u>verified</u> findings made through the <u>telescope</u>.

One day, alas, his spaceship crashed; his fine equipment all was trashed.

He went out to <u>inspect</u> the mess, and think and probe and <u>judge</u> and guess and <u>prospect</u> for some things of worth, so he could travel back to Earth.

<u>Prognosticating</u> by the moon, he hoped that he could get back soon.

Employing <u>scientific</u> means, he built a worthy craft, it seems.

For he arrived back yesterday, and left to vacation in Paraguay.

But soon he'll be back out in space, exploring some new distant place.

Set # 94, page 227

Greek

"not knowing"	agnostic
"without leadership"	anarchy
"against the law; opposition"	antinomy
"rule by a single person"	autocracy
"to talk together"	dialogue
"a pleasant way of speaking about an unpleasant topic"	euphemism

"overcritical"	hypercritical
"an instrument that enlarges a small sound"	microphone
"beyond opinion"	paradox
"an instrument that allows one to look around corners"	periscope
"with a false appearance of refinement"	pseudo-sophisticated

Latin

"having two lenses, for both eyes"	binoculars
"to look around; prudent"	circumspect
"to reduce the value of"	devalue
"able to speak many languages"	multilingual
"to evaluate before sufficient evidence is available"	prejudge
"to look at again in order to correct"	revision
"to make move again"	reanimate
"to make live again"	revive
"letting light shine through"	translucent
"to breathe out"	transpire

CHAPTER TEN

Predictable Spelling Changes: Changes in Sight

NOW YOU SEE IT, NOW YOU DON'T

In Chapter 7 we talked about alternations—changes in sound when spelling stayed the same. Now we're going to discuss changes in spelling that come about mainly to make words more pronounceable. When we add affixes to roots, sometimes the result is kind of hard to say. We accommodate these situations with little shifts that help us get our tongues around what we're trying to say.

Look at these suffix additions and try saying the results without and with the accommodation. Which works best, do you think?

Root + Suffix	Result without Accommodation	Pronunciation	Result with Accommodation
erode + sion	erodsion	/ir ōd sh∂n/	erosion
comprehend + sion	comprehendsion	/kōm prĭ hĕnd sh∂n/	comprehension
introduce + tion	introducetion	/ĭn tr∂ do͞os sh∂n/	introduction
magic + ian	magician	/mă jĭk sh∂n/	magician

WOW!

Better, right?

_e r o s i o n

Remember this? Changes at the syllable juncture

Remember how we dealt with some spelling changes to match sound changes when we added /ən/? Then we were differentiating /ən/ endings. Now we're going to focus on the spelling changes that happen when these suffixes are added.

D and DE changes

erode *de* spells /d/ → erosion *s(i)* spells /zh/

comprehend *d* spells /d/ → comprehension *s(i)* spells /sh/

CE changes

introduce *ce* spells /s/ → introduction *c* spells /k/

C changes

magic *c* spells /k/ → magician *ci* spells /sh/

BRAIN TICKLERS
Set # 95

Write the *-ion* or *-ian* form of each word given below. Group the resulting words into the groups represented in the chart above:

D → S   CE → C
DE → S   C → CI

collide	include	politic
decide	invade	produce
delude	mathematics	reduce
explode	music	statistic
extend	persuade	

(Answers are on page 249.)

What's happening to my vowels?

Sometimes adding a suffix changes things beyond the syllable juncture. Yes, back in the middle of the word, things can change, too. Remember how adding a suffix can change pronunciation? We talked about these alternations in Chapter 7. Often, these changes were either from or to a schwa sound, and since schwa can be spelled with virtually any vowel letter, the spelling didn't change.

Now we're getting to the more sophisticated stuff. And the fact is, sometimes the sound AND the spelling change. Remember the word *morpheme*? It's the smallest unit of language that has meaning and cannot be subdivided. However, a single morpheme can have more than one shape. Here's an example:

vain in *vain* and **van** in *vanity* are the same morpheme. The long *a* spelled *ai* becomes an *a*, and the vowel sound changes from long to short. In adding the suffix *-ity* to a word like *insane*, dropping the *e* is enough to signal the change from a long to a short vowel sound. No other spelling change is needed.

sume in *consume* and **sump** in *consumption* are also the same morpheme. The long *u* marked by the final *e* changes to a *u* followed by a double consonant, indicating a short pronunciation—again, a change from long to short. Notice that in both cases, the accented syllable remains the same.

When you have more than one visual/sound form of a morpheme, the multiple forms are called *allomorphs*.

Some allomorphs have a long version and a schwa version for when the accentuation changes syllables. Since schwa is hardly ever spelled with a double vowel (*ou* is the only case that comes to mind), the spelling changes as well. So we get:

explain′ → explana′tion **plain → plan** and the accent moves to the following syllable

exclaim′ → exclama′tion **claim → clam** and the accent moves to the following syllable

Notice how the initial vowel stays the same—the vowel with which the sound is named—and the second vowel is dropped.

BRAIN TICKLER
Set # 96

Given the examples above, predict the vowel change for each bold syllable when adding the suffix indicated. Then write the word with the suffix. Use a dictionary if you need to.

re**ceive** + tion   **bile** + ious
per**ceive** + tion   **grain** + ular
de**ceive** + tion   **mime** + ic
state + ic   **flame** + able
tone + ic

(Answers are on page 249.)

ASSIMILATION INVESTIGATION— MEET THE CHAMELEONS

And I thought I knew a thing or two about assimilation!

Now we're going to wind up our exploration of spelling with the most changeable of all morphemes: a set of prefixes that change their final consonant in order to better fit with the root or base word they attach to. Just like a chameleon that changes its color to match its surroundings, these guys change their shape to better fit in with whatever follows—to smooth out the syllable juncture, as it were. This can make them tricky to recognize, because they look one way one time, and a different way the next time— these prefixes have more allomorphs than you can shake a stick at. So let's start off by meeting them.

The basic six

Here they are:

Prefix	Meaning(s)
ad	to, toward
in	not, into
com	with
ob	against, toward
sub	under
syn	together, with

BRAIN TICKLERS
Set # 97

Write the meaning of each word. (Note: you're going to find some unusual words here, because we're going to use only bases that are words.) Use a dictionary if you need to. Note how the affix joins onto the word.

ad	adjoin	administer
in	incapable	insufficient
com	commingle	compromise
ob	(no base word examples)	
sub	submarine	subsoil
syn	synoptic	synchronic

(Answers are on page 249.)

Ad it up

There are ELEVEN allomorphs for *ad* (including *ad* itself). The prefix *ad* turns to *a-* before *sc*, *sp*, *st*, and *gn*. Otherwise, *ad*'s consonant matches the consonant it precedes.

Allomorph	Sample Word
ac	accompany
acq	acquaintance
ad	adjoin
af	affirm
ag	aggrieve
al	allot
an	annotate
ar	arrest
as	assort
at	attune

How do you know if it's an allomorph of *ad-* or some other morpheme? Look at the etymology in the dictionary entry. For example, if you look up *accompany* and look at the etymology all the way back to the origins of the word, it will say something like *ad* + compain(g). That *ad* in the etymology tells you that *ac* is an allomorph of *ad*.

Did you notice how many doubled consonants there are at the syllable juncture of the prefix and the root or base word, like in *accompany*? That's one of the signs of an assimilated prefix.

BRAIN TICKLERS
Set # 98

Find one example of a word for each allomorph of *ad*. It can be attached to a base word or a root word.

(Answers are on page 250.)

In at the beginning

There are five allomorphs of *in-*.

Allomorph of *in*	Sample Word
i (before *g*)	ignominy
il (before *l*)	illegal
im (before *b*, *m*, *p*)	immortal
ir (before *r*)	irrational
in (the rest of the time)	incapable

BRAIN TICKLERS
Set # 99

Find two examples of words for each allo-morph of *in*. They can be attached to a base word or a root word. How many of the ten have a doubled consonant at the syllable junc-ture between the prefix and the root or base word?

(Answers are on page 250.)

Don't let *com* con you

	Sample Word
Before *b*, *p*, and *m*, it's *com*.	complain
Before *h*, *g*, *n*, and usually before vowels, it's *co*.	cogent
Before *i*, it's *col* and before *r*, it's *cor*.	collaborate/corroborate
Before other consonants, it's *con*.	conjecture

BRAIN TICKLERS
Set # 100

Find a word for each allomorph of *com* and use them to write a poem.

(Answers are on page 250.)

Toward an understanding of *ob*

o before *m*	omit
oc before *c*	occur
of before *f*	offend
op before *p*	oppose
ob the rest of the time	observe

Sub-pose we learn about *sub*

Sub is not just for submarines! Take a look.

suc before *c*	succeed
suf before *f*	suffix
sug before *g*	suggest
sum before *m*	summon
sup before *p*	suppose
sur before *r*	surreptitious
sus sometimes before *c, p, t*	suspect
sub before all else	submarine

BRAIN TICKLERS
Set # 101

Find a *sub* or *ob* word to match each clue. A hint tells you which allomorph to use for each.

1. Under the basement (*sub*)
2. No longer in use (*ob*)
3. Brief and clear (*suc*)
4. To enslave (*op*)
5. To maintain (*sus*)
6. To make something available (*sup*)

(Answers are on page 250.)

Syn is with us

Last one. Are you ready?

sym before *b, m, p*	sympathy
syl before *i*	syllable
sy before *s* and *z*	system
syn elsewhere	syntax

BRAIN TICKLERS
Set # 102

Match the words with the definitions.

Words

1. syllogism
2. symphony
3. synchronize
4. syncretism
5. syndrome

6. syzygy

Clues

a. set of signs that indicates a disease
b. combining of different belief systems
c. to happen in unison
d. long sonata for orchestra
e. point at which a celestial body is in conjunction with the sun
f. reasoning from the general to the specific

And on that excellent spelling bee word—syzygy—we end.

(Answers are on page 251.)

BRAIN TICKLERS— THE ANSWERS

Set # 95, page 238

D → s
extension
DE → s

collision	explosion	persuasion
decision	inclusion	
delusion	invasion	

CE → c

production	reduction

C → ci

mathematician	politician
musician	statistician

Set # 96, page 240

re**ceive** + tion	*e*	reception
per**ceive** + tion	*e*	preception
de**ceive** +tion	*e*	deception
state + ic	drop *e*	static
tone + ic	drop *e*	tonic
bile + ious	drop *e*	bilious
grain + ular	drop *i*	granular
mime + ic	drop *e*	mimic
flame +able	drop *e*	flammable

Set # 97, page 242

adjoin	to be next to
administer	to direct
incapable	not capable
insufficient	not sufficient
commingle	to mingle with
compromise	to settle differences with
submarine	a ship that can operate beneath the water
subsoil	the layer of earth under the topsoil
synoptic	presenting a report from the same point of view
synchronic	occurring at the same time

Set # 98, page 244

Possible response:

a ascend	**af** affix	**ar** arrange
ac accustom	**ag** aggravate	**as** assimilate
acq acquire	**al** allocate	**at** attend
ad admire	**an** announce	

Set # 99, page 245

Possible response:

i   ignore, ignoble
in inaccurate, inappropriate
il illegible, illuminate
im immaterial, immature
ir irresponsible, irregular

Six have a doubled consonant.

Set # 100, page 246

Possible response:

co coexist	**com** compare
col collect	**con** construct conclude (one extra!)
cor correct	

How can I <u>construct</u> a poem that makes sense
When I'm feeling rather dense?
How many allomorphs must I <u>collect</u>?
It's hard to get them all <u>correct</u>.
Why should so many forms <u>coexist</u>?
I have to keep adding to my list.
When each prefix I <u>compare,</u>
I just <u>conclude</u> it isn't fair.

Set # 101, page 247

1. subbasement
2. obsolete
3. succinct
4. oppress
5. sustain
6. supply

Set # 102, page 248

1. f
2. d
3. c
4. b
5. a
6. e

INDEX

Really. This isn't going to hurt at all . . .

Barron's *Painless* titles are perfect ways to show kids in middle school that learning really doesn't hurt. They'll even discover that grammar, algebra, and other subjects that many of them consider boring can become fascinating— and yes, even fun! The trick is in the presentation: clear instruction, taking details one step at a time, adding a light and humorous touch, and sprinkling in some brain-tickler puzzles that are both challenging and entertaining to solve.

Each book: Paperback, approx. 224 pp., $8.95, Canada $11.95

Painless Algebra
Lynette Long, Ph.D.
Confusing algebraic terms are translated into simple English, then presented step by step, with a touch of humor and a brain tickler in every chapter.
ISBN 0-7641-0676-7

Painless American History
Curt Lader
Timelines, ideas for fascinating Internet projects, and the author's light narrative style are just a few of the ingredients that make this American History book one that kids will <u>enjoy</u> reading.
ISBN 0-7641-0620-1

Painless Fractions
Alyece Cummings
Fractions become easy when you learn some simple rules. Problems, puns, puzzles, and more—all with answers.
ISBN 0-7641-0445-4

Painless Grammar
Rebecca S. Elliott, Ph.D.
Here's a book that takes the dryness out of nouns, verbs, adjectives, and adverbs. Kids also analyze some of the wackier words in the English language.
ISBN 0-8120-5056-1

Painless Research Projects
Rebecca S. Elliott, Ph.D., and James Elliott, M.A.
The secret is to choose an interesting project. Here's advice on how to find one, then get started, and follow up with research and report-writing.
ISBN 0-7641-0297-4

Painless Science Projects
Faith Hickman Brynie, Ph.D.
The author insists that doing a science project can be fun. Then she proves it by demonstrating how to begin: Ask good science questions—the kind that produce fascinating answers!
ISBN 0-7641-0595-7

Painless Spelling
Mary Elizabeth Podhaizer
Spelling correctly becomes easy once you learn some basic rules, discover how to analyze sound patterns, and explore word origins.
ISBN 0-7641-0567-1

Barron's Educational Series, Inc.
250 Wireless Boulevard, Hauppauge, NY 11788
In Canada: Georgetown Book Warehouse
34 Armstrong Avenue, Georgetown, Ont. L7G 4R9
Visit our Web Site @ www.barronseduc.com
(#79) 6/99